101 Language Arts Activities

by Trudy Aarons, Francine Koelsch

Games, Gameboards and Learning Centers
for Early Childhood Education
and Special Needs Children

**Communication
Skill Builders, Inc.** ✱®
3130 N. Dodge Blvd./P.O. Box 42050
Tucson, Arizona 85733
(602) 327-6021

Education Curriculum

FROM THE PUBLISHER:

PEEL & PUT® pressure-sensitive pictures illustrating sounds can be used in the following 42 games detailed in *101 Language Arts Activities:*

Games require duplicate sets

PEEL & PUT® programs are described in our free catalog, which is available upon request. A PEEL & PUT® pictures selection containing 500 full-color, uniform, pressure-sensitive pictures (25 sheets) plus 2 alphabet sheets and 1 shapes/visual closure sheet is available for $29 (CSB catalog no. 2017).

Copyright © 1979 by **Communication Skill Builders, Inc.**
3130 N. Dodge Blvd./P.O. Box 42050
Tucson, Arizona 85733

ISBN 0-88450-795-5
Catalog No. 3053

INTRODUCTION

101 Language Arts Activities is an outgrowth of necessity. Several years ago as kindergarten teachers, we participated in a Title I Grant. This involved sending home a weekly "Smiley Bag" project with each child. Limited to commercially bought games and activities, we found they did not fill our students' needs since there were many gaps in their skills that needed development and reinforcement. Using our creativity and embellishing upon ideas from fellow teachers, we began to make many games that filled the language arts needs of our students. The games were made from available and inexpensive materials. As word of our games and activities circulated, we were invited to conduct several workshops to teacher groups, as well as parent groups. These workshops were very successful since all participants were able to produce as many games as time permitted. During the workshops, many teachers and parents requested a book of games for young children. This request started us writing *101 Language Arts Activities*.

The book is unique in that the majority of the games can be used by a child who cannot decode words. The games under each category are sequenced from the easiest skills to the more difficult skills. Before the game is introduced to the class or the individual child, the skill must be matched to the child's readiness level. Each activity states the title of the game, the objective, the materials used, making the game, and playing the game.

We hope you have as much fun making the games as your children will have in using them.

ACKNOWLEDGEMENTS

To our husbands
Fred and Howell
for their steadfast encouragement and patience.

To our children
Jason and Justin
Beth, Wendy, Ellen, and Marci
for their help in making and experimenting with the activities.

HOW TO BEGIN

Beginnings can be the hardest part of a project. To help you begin, we've listed the materials that have worked best for us, and some avoidable pitfalls.

Materials

★ Folding bristol works best for table gameboards and card games. It is flexible and sturdy; it comes in an assortment of colors and sizes.

★ Bristol board is heavier than folding bristol. It is excellent for wall and bulletin board learning stations, and for large floor games.

★ Water-based marking pens are colorful and will make your games attractive. Never use any permanent type of marking pen. They have an oil base that will eventually cause the colors to "bleed."

★ Clear adhesive plastic is a must to cover all your games if you wish them to last any length of time.

★ Pictures for your games can be found in seals, workbooks, and there are companies that have language arts pictures. Try your Speech and Language Clinician for a catalog.

Avoidable Pitfalls

★ When you make a game with cards, cut the cards apart after you have covered the game with plastic.

★ Paper-punch a hole in the end of the pointer when making a spinner. Place a paper fastener through the hole and push it through the spinner. Loosen up the fastener and it will spin freely.

★ Make sure the children have all the necessary entry behaviors in order to play the game. Demonstrate how to play the activity in front of the group before putting out the game.

★ Establish a routine with your class for using the activities. For example: (1) the correct number of players, (2) completing the activity before choosing another, (3) checking with the teacher when the activity is completed, (4) putting away the activity.

★ Storage of the activity is important. Each activity should have a specific place it belongs. It should be visible to the children, and within their reach. Pieces of the activity should be kept together.

CONTENTS

Visual Discrimination

PEEK AND CHECK

Objective

To select the picture that is different

Materials

1. Bristol board
2. Hole punch
3. Stickers
4. Scissors
5. Pencil
6. Red marking pen
7. Self–adhesive clear plastic

Making the Game

1. Cut the bristol board 3'' x 12''.
2. Paste stickers on the strip at approximately every 2½'' interval. Three will be alike, one different.
3. Punch a hole under each sticker.
4. Color code the different sticker on the back of the strip.
5. Cover with clear plastic. Punch out the covered hole.
6. This project can be made using numbers, letters, colors, and words.

Playing the Game

1. The child will look at all the pictures on the card.
2. The child will select the picture that is different from the others.
3. He/she will put a pencil in the hole under the picture that is different.
4. He/she will turn the card over to see if the hole is red coded. If it is red coded it is correct.

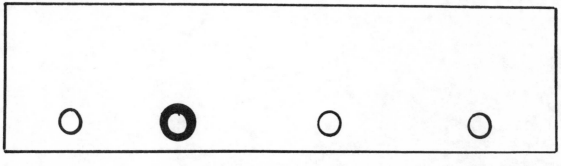

reverse
side

WHERE'S MY HALF?

Objective

To see the relationship of the part to the whole

Materials

1. Bristol board, folding

2. Assortment of pictures with a single item on them

3. Clear adhesive plastic

Making the Game

1. Rule the cards 3" x 3" or 3" x 4". Place the picture in the center of the card. Cover the cards with plastic.

2. Cut each card in half.

Playing the Game

1. Begin with a deck of 12 pairs of cards. Deal them face down in rows. First player turns over two cards. If they match and make a whole picture, he keeps the cards and continues turning over two at a time until he cannot find a match. The player with the most whole pictures at the end is the winner.

2. The cards may be used to play an "Old Maid" type of game. Each player is given four cards. Before play begins, he sorts his cards to see if he has a match. Each time he makes a match he draws a card from the remaining deck which is face down in the center.

   The first player draws one card from the hand of the second player. If the card matches one in the hand, the player lays down the match and draws a card from the center pile. The play moves around the circle, with players taking turns drawing cards from others' hands. The player with the most whole sets wins.

CATCH THE FISH

Objective

To match colors

Materials

1. Two wooden dowels
2. String
3. Two magnets
4. Construction paper
5. Scissors
6. Clear adhesive plastic
7. Cardboard box
8. Paint
9. Paper clips

Making the Game

1. Paint the cardboard carton.

2. Make fishing poles with the dowels, string, and magnets.

3. Cut fish from a variety of colored construction paper, having at least two of every color. Cover each one with clear adhesive.

4. Place a paper clip on each fish, then put in the carton.

Playing the Game

1. Two players take a turn fishing for two fish.

2. If the fish captured match in color, the player keeps the fish.

3. After all the fish are caught, the player with the most fish is the winner.

4. Variations may be fishing for shapes or pictures.

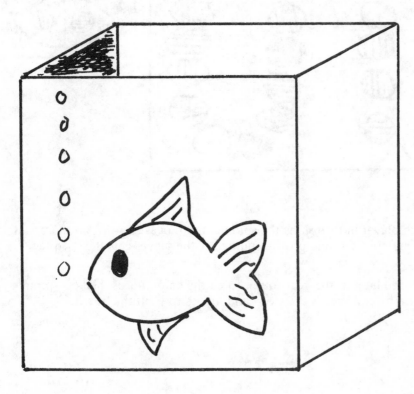

magnet

COLOR WALK

Objective

To develop color discriminations

Materials

1. Folding bristol 12" x 18", and 7" x 7", white

2. Marking pens, ruler, paper fastener, hole punch

3. Clear adhesive plastic

Making the Game

1. Choose five basic colors. Draw a 6" diameter circle on the 7" square paper, and divide it into six sections. Place a color in each section and a sad face in the sixth section. Cover with plastic. Make a pointer; punch a hole in the end of the pointer and attach it to the spinner with the fastener.

2. Follow the illustration to make your game board path. Repeat the five colors eight times, alternating the order. Cover the board with plastic.

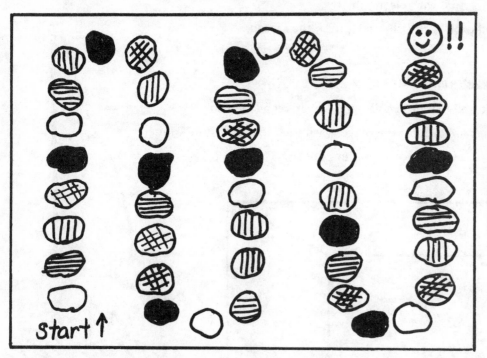 

Playing the Game

1. Beginning at the start, each player in turn spins the spinner and moves forward on the board to the nearest color that matches the one on the spinner. If the player gets the "sad face," he loses his turn.

2. This game board may be used later in the year to reinforce the color words. Make a spinner with the color words on it. The child reads the word and moves to it on the board.

COLOR LACE

Objective

To match colors and color words

Materials

1. Cardboard or bristol
2. Hole punch or pointed scissors
3. Shoelaces
4. Colored marking pens
5. Clear adhesive plastic

Making the Game

1. Cut the cardboard to desired size.
2. With various colored marking pens, make circles on the left and right sides of the board (card 1). Card 2 will have the circles on the left and color-coded words on the right. Card 3 will have circles on the left and color names on the right.
3. Cover the boards with clear adhesive plastic.
4. Punch holes next to the circles or words. Put a lace in each hole on the left side. Knot the lace in the back.

Playing the Game

1. The child will match the same colors by connecting the lace to the corresponding color (card 1).
2. The child will match the colors with the color-coded words (card 2).
3. The player will match the color word and the corresponding color with the laces.

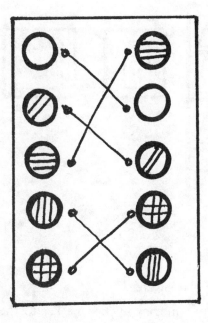 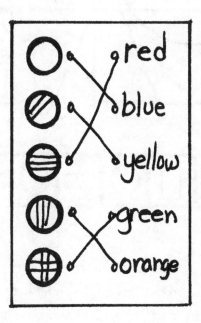

Card 2. Words are color-coded

Card 3. Words are in black

MATCH THE SHAPE

Objective

To match shapes and colors

Materials

1. Cardboard game board
2. Shape stickers
3. Colored marking pens
4. Bristol
5. Game markers

Making the Game

1. Cut the bristol into small cards.
2. Make a game board of shapes. Use identical shapes on the small cards.
3. Cover the board and cards with clear adhesive plastic.

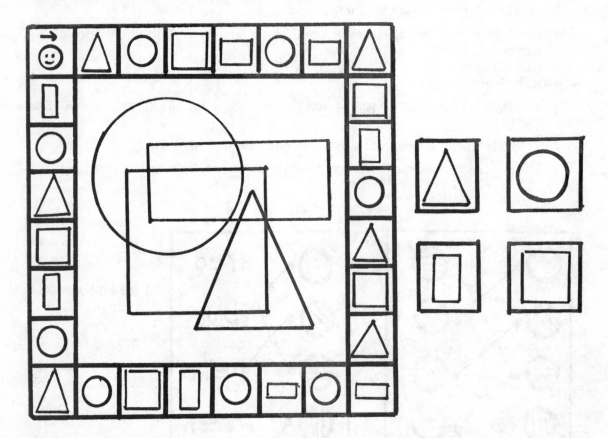

Playing the Game

1. Two or more players are needed for the game.
2. The small cards are placed face down in the middle of the playing area.
3. Each player takes a turn picking a card from the pile, then moving his/her marker to the shape that matches the card.
4. The players advance on the gameboard, matching the shapes picked. The first player to reach the end is the winner.

SHAPE RACE

Objective

To match shapes of the same color

Materials

1. Cardboard game board

2. Shape stickers or small shape pictures

3. Marking pens

4. Spinner

5. Game markers

Making the Game

1. Make a spinner board of different colored shapes.

2. Make a game board of shapes used on the spinner board, alternating the shapes and colors.

Playing the Game

1. Two players are needed for the game.

2. Player no. 1 spins the spinner, then proceeds to place his/her marker on the shape.

3. The game continues with each player taking a turn until a player reaches the smiling face.

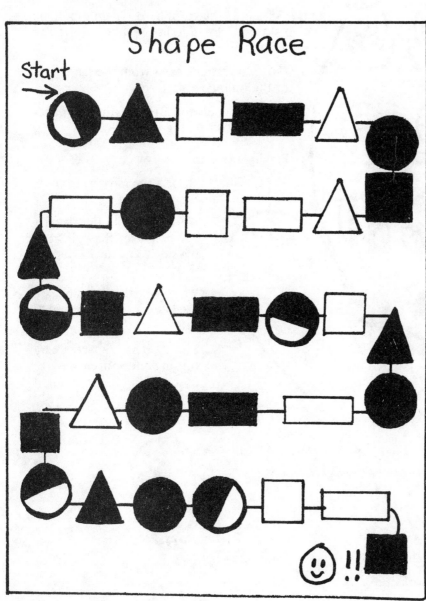

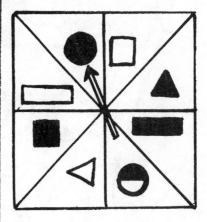

MATCH THE MITTENS

Objective

To match patterns

Materials

1. Wallpaper
2. Scissors
3. 18" x 24" cardboard or bristol
4. Marking pens
5. Container for the mittens

Making the Game

1. Cut the cardboard into the shape of a mitten.

2. Cut slits into the cardboard. There should be two slits side-by-side in order to receive the matched pairs.

3. Cut two mittens each from the same page of the wallpaper pattern.

4. Color code the back of the wallpaper for self-checking.

Playing the Game

1. The child sorts the mittens from its container.

2. When the child finds a pair, he/she places the pair side-by-side on the cardboard slits.

3. When all the mittens are used there will be no more slits.

4. The child can self-check by turning the mitten over to observe the same colored circles.

color-coded reverse side

GO AGAIN

Objective

> To see likenesses

Materials

1. Folding bristol
2. White glue
3. 12 sets of pictures, 2 identical pictures in a set
4. Clear adhesive plastic

Making the Game

1. Rule the paper into 3'' x 4'' cards. Place a picture on each card. Cover the cards with plastic before you cut them apart.

Playing the Game

1. Each player receives three cards. The rest of the deck is placed face down in the center. First player asks the second player if he has a matching card. If the second player does, he must give his card to the first player, who then makes a "pack" of the two matching cards and places them aside. The first player "goes again" until he cannot match a card in his hand. Then he takes a card from the center deck, and the second player tries to match a card in his hand. The game is over when all the cards are matched. A player draws from the face-down deck if he uses all his cards. Player with the most packs wins.

2. This deck of cards may be used for "concentration" game, where all the cards are placed face down and the players turn two cards over at a time, looking for a match.

PICTURE LOTTO

Objective

To develop visual discrimination and observation skills

Materials

1. Folding bristol
2. Assortment of pictures, 2 of each
3. Ruler, marking pens, paper cutter
4. Clear adhesive plastic

Making the Game

1. Rule the lotto cards 9"x 9" or 6" x 9". Put a picture in each square. No two cards should have the same picture.
2. The stimulus cards will be ruled 3" x 3" or 2" x 3" depending on the size of your lotto cards. Put the matching pictures on the cards.
3. Cover the lotto cards and the stimulus cards with plastic before you cut them apart with the paper cutter.

Playing the Game

1. Shuffle the deck of cards and place it face down in the middle of the playing area. Give each player a lotto card. Each player in turn draws the top card from the deck. If it matches a picture on any player's card, he places it on. If it does not match anyone's card, it is placed on the discard pile. The game ends when a player covers his card.

2. Your lotto cards may have any variety of pictures. Colors, actions, shapes, sizes, positions, foods, objects, clothing, toys, etc.

RACE TO WIN

Objective

To see likenesses

Materials

1. Folding bristol, 12'' x 18'', and 7'' x 7''
2. Marking pens, ruler, paper fastener, hole punch
3. Clear adhesive plastic
4. Six sets of pictures, seven identical pictures in each set

Making the Game

1. Cut a square of bristol 7'' x 7'' for the spinner. Draw a 6'' diameter circle in the center. Divide it into six sections and place a different picture in each section. Cover with plastic. Make a pointer. Punch a hole in the end of the pointer and attach it to the spinner with the paper fastener.
2. Follow the illustration to make your game board path. You will repeat the pictures on the spinner six times, alternating the order. Cover the game board with plastic.

Playing the Game

1. Beginning at the start, each player in turn spins the spinner and moves forward on the board to the nearest picture that matches the one on the spinner.
2. Instead of a spinner, you may use a set of cards with the matching pictures on them. You would need three picture cards for every picture on the spinner. Reshuffle the deck when you turn over the last card.

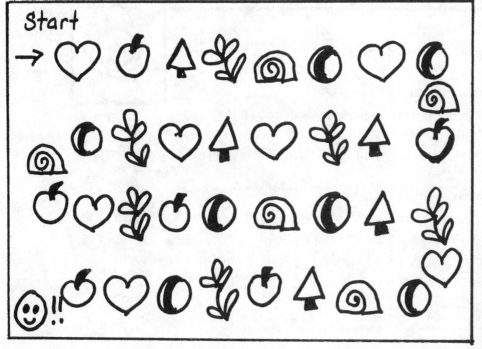

PICTURE TRAIN

Objective

To match pictures that are the same

Materials

1. Bristol board
2. Marking pen
3. Stickers or small pictures with duplicates
4. Clear adhesive plastic

Making the Game

1. Cut the cards to size, 2" x 4".
2. Make a line at the 2" mark to designate the halves.
3. Apply the stickers on each half or draw a picture on each half.
4. After applying pictures on each half, cover the cards with clear adhesive plastic.

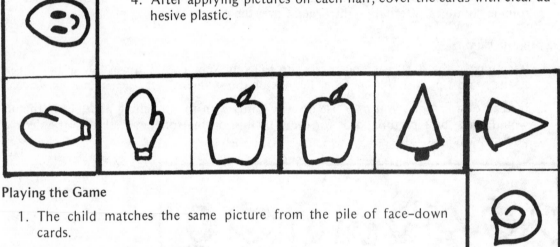

Playing the Game

1. The child matches the same picture from the pile of face-down cards.
2. One player selects a card one at a time.
3. He/she puts the matches together. If there is no match on the table he/she can keep the card until a match can be made.
4. The next player continues by taking turns in trying to make matches with the drawn cards.
5. All cards touching must be the same.
6. The player with no cards or the least number of cards at the end of the game is the winner.

POST OFFICE

Objective

To develop object discrimination

Materials

1. Folding bristol
2. Bristol board
3. Two identical assortments of pictures
4. Marking pens, ruler, scissors, small drapery hooks
5. Clear plastic

Making the Game

1. Following the illustration, make a set of mailboxes, 9" x 12" from the heavier bristol board. Write a name and an address on the side of the mailbox; and place a picture on the box.

2. Make a set of envelopes from the folding bristol. On each copy, write the name and address from a mailbox and place on it a matching picture.

3. Cover the mailboxes and the letters with plastic.

Playing the Game

1. The child sets the mailboxes along the chalkboard or face up on the table. He/she matches the letters to the mailboxes by matching the pictures.

2. For a more difficult task, make a second set of letters or envelopes with only the matching names and addresses. This activity would be for those children with the necessary entry behaviors.

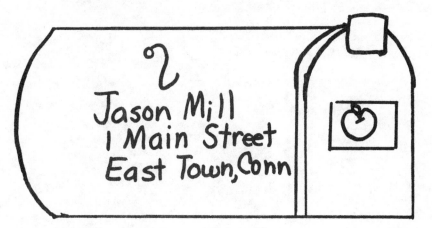

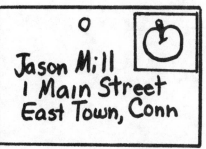

Visual Memory

PICTURES, PICTURES

Objective

To develop non–sequential visual memory

Materials

1. Folding bristol, 9" x 12" or 12" x 18"

2. Two identical picture assortments of familiar things

3. Clear adhesive plastic

Making the Game

1. Place between 8 to 12 pictures on the paper in random order. Cover the board with plastic.

2. For each board you make, make a set of matching cards. Rule the bristol into 3"x 3" cards. Put the matching pictures on the cards. Cover the cards with plastic before you cut them apart.

Playing the Game

1. Show the picture to the group for 12 seconds. Ask the first player to name all the things he/she remembers. As he/she recalls items, place the card of the named item on the back of the large picture which is face down in the center. Ask other members if they can remember additional items. Show the picture again and match the cards named to the items in the picture.

2. Repeat the game with a different picture and a different child until everyone has had a turn.

SHOPPING LIST

Objective

To develop non-sequential visual memory

Materials

1. Folding bristol

2. Two identical assortments of pictures and logos

3. Small lunch bags

4. Clear adhesive plastic

Making the Game

1. For the shopping lists, rule the paper into 9" x 3" sections. Follow the illustrations and make sets of lists that have three items, four items, five items, and six items. The actual number of items you use depends on the group's development in visual memory. You may wish to make lists with more than six items.

2. Rule the paper into 4" x 4" squares. Put the matching pictures on the cards.

3. Cover the shopping lists and the purchase cards with plastic.

Playing the Game

1. Show the first member of the group his/her shopping list. Have him/her read back the items. Turn his/her list face down on the table and send him/her to the "store" with a shopping bag. The "store" will be the area where you have the purchase cards displayed. The player will select his/her items, put them in a bag, bring them back to the group, and compare his/her purchases with the list.

2. Begin play with the three-item sets of shopping lists. Increase the number of items on the list gradually.

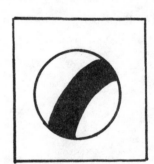

NAME THEM

Objective

To develop non–sequential visual memory

Materials

1. Folding bristol
2. Assortment of pictures and small items
3. A container — "Pringles" chip can, covered box
4. Clear adhesive plastic

Making the Game

1. Put the pictures on 3" x 3" cards and cover with plastic.
2. Cover the container with decorative paper (wallpaper, wrapping paper, funny papers, finger paint paper) and cover it with plastic.

Playing the Game

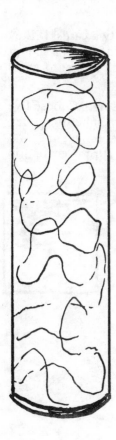

1. Place the pictures and the objects on the table. Choose one member of the group to put things in the container. He/she names the items as he/she places them in the container. The other members of the group take turns naming one item in the container. After naming them, the container is emptied to see if all the items were named.

2. Another version of the game would be to have one member of the group close his/her eyes while members of the group place pictures and items in the container. The player would then try to remember what is missing from the remaining pictures. The number of things placed in the container would depend on the skill level of the group.

CARD CONCENTRATION

Objective

To develop visual memory

Materials

1. Folding bristol

2. Two identical sets of pictures

3. Clear adhesive plastic

Making the Game

1. Rule the cards into 3" x 3" squares. Put a picture in each square. You will want to start with twelve pairs of cards.

2. Cover the cards with plastic before you cut them apart.

Playing the Game

1. Put the cards face down in rows on the table. The first player turns over two cards. If they match, he/she keeps them and continues turning two cards over at a time until he/she cannot find a matching pair. The player must replace the cards that do not match in their original spot. The player with the most pairs wins.

2. A second game to play with these cards would be a form of "what's missing." Choose five pairs of cards. Put the pairs in duplicate rows, face up. Have the group remember the order. Turn the top row of cards face down. Mix up the bottom row of cards and have the first player lay them down in the original order below the top face-down row. Turn over the top row of cards to check for the correct order.

STRING THOSE BEADS

Objective

To develop sequential visual memory

Materials

1. White folding bristol

2. Marking pens

3. Clear adhesive plastic

4. Set of wooden beads, assorted colors, sizes, shapes

Making the Game

1. Rule the paper into 3'' x 6'' rectangles.

2. Make clue cards, working from the easiest skill to the most difficult. The first sets should have one variable — one color, one size, different shape; one shape, one size, different color; one shape, one color, different size. The first sets should also have only two to four beads to remember.

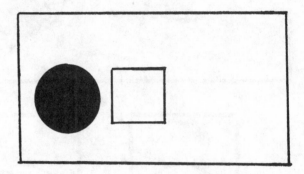

3. The more advanced level will have two or three variables — one size, different colors, different shapes, etc.

4. Make your clue cards with the marking pens. Cover the cards with plastic before you cut them apart.

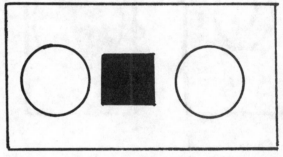

Playing the Game

1. Put the set of clue cards face down. The player turns over the top card, remembers it, turns it face down. He/she then strings the beads and compares it with the clue card.

2. For a more advanced level, the child continues to repeat the pattern on his/her string until all the beads in the set are used.

REMEMBER, REMEMBER

Objective

To develop sequential visual memory

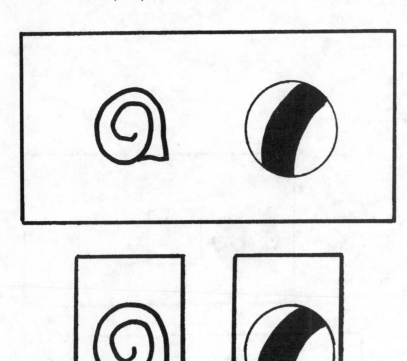

Materials

1. Folding bristol, 12" x 18"

2. Assortment of pictures; six designs with eight of each design

3. Clear adhesive plastic

Making the Game

1. Rule the paper into rectangles, 3" x 6". Divide two rectangles into 2" x 3" rectangles.

2. Put one picture of each design into the six smallest rectangles. These will be the clue cards.

3. Put one, two or three pictures in each remaining rectangle. Do not repeat a sequence or duplicate a card.

4. Cover the cards with plastic before you cut them apart.

Playing the Game

1. Place the six small cards face up in a row in front of the player. Place the large cards face down in a pile.

2. Turn up the top card. The player memorizes the pictures then turns the card face down. He/she then chooses from the small clue cards; the one he/she thinks will duplicate the large card. He/she moves the small cards below the large card, and turns the large card over for the check.

FOR MY BIRTHDAY

Objective

To develop sequential memory skills

Materials

1. Folding bristol

2. Assortment of pictures

3. Clear adhesive plastic

Making the Game

1. Rule the paper into 3" x 3" squares. Put a picture in each square.

2. Cover the cards with plastic before you cut them apart.

Playing the Game

1. Put the deck of cards face down in the center of play. The first player turns over the top card and says, "For my birthday I want . . ." and names the card. He/she places the card face up. The second player turns over a card from the deck and says, "For my birthday I want . . ." and names the first card and then his/her card. The play continues until all the players have turned over a card.

2. For the second round of play, the first player turns a card face down. Now he/she names all the cards in order, beginning with his/her card that is now face down. All the players name the cards in turn. The second player then turns his/her card face down. Now the group, in turn, recalls all the cards in order, beginning with the first two cards which are now face down. This continues until all the players' cards are face down, and each player has had a turn recalling the face-down cards.

3. The number of cards used depends on the skill level of the group.

WHAT'S MISSING?

Objective

To develop recall

Materials

1. Folding bristol
2. Assortment of pictures
3. Clear adhesive plastic

Making the Game

1. Rule the paper into 3" x 3" squares. Put a picture in each square.
2. Cover the cards with plastic before you cut them apart.

Playing the Game

1. Have the players name the pictures as you line them up on the table. Have one player close his/her eyes, and take away one picture. Have him/her tell you what is missing.
2. For a more advanced play, take more than one item away and ask the player to name all the pictures that are missing.
3. Change the order of the pictures and have the player put the pictures back in the original sequence.

Auditory Discrimination

WHERE AM I?

Objective

To tell from which part of the room a sound is heard

Materials

Musical instruments, such as: triangles, bells, sticks, or wood blocks

Making the Game

1. Gather all musical instruments that produce a variety of sounds.

2. Place them on a table in front of the children.

Playing the Game

1. Children sit in a semicircle.

2. One child is chosen to produce a sound. The others close their eyes.

3. The leader chooses an instrument. He/she tiptoes to the front, back, etc., of the room, then plays the instrument. He/she tiptoes back to the group.

4. The leader tells the children to open their eyes. One child is chosen to tell where the sound came from and/or which instrument was heard. If correct, he/she is the leader.

5. Another variety of play may be to work with one child at a time by having that child hide his/her eyes. The others would watch until that child guesses; then another child is chosen.

SHAKE IT

Objective

   To match sounds that are the same

Materials

   1. Ten plastic medicine containers or film containers — each must be the same size

   2. Paint

   3. Materials to fill the containers, such as salt, rice, pegs, or beans

Making the Game

   1. Paint the medicine containers so they are no longer clear.

   2. Fill two containers with the same materials.

   3. When shaking the containers, the sounds must match.

   4. Proceed with the others until you have five matching.

   5. Color-code the containers and put them all in a box.

Playing the Game

   1. The child selects two bottles from the box.

   2. Holding the top and bottom of the bottle, he/she shakes the container. If the sounds match, he/she makes a pair.

   3. Proceed with the other containers until there are five pairs. The child can self-check the pairs by looking at the color-coding on the bottom of the container.

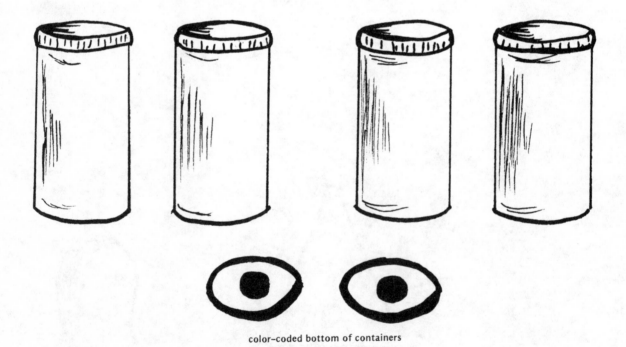

color-coded bottom of containers

THE MUFFIN MAN

Objective

To name the person singing "Do you Know the Muffin Man?" without seeing the singer

Materials

1. Chair in front of the room
2. Blindfold (optional)
3. Piano accompaniment (optional)

Making the Game

Gather materials necessary to play the game.

Playing the Game

1. A child is chosen to sit in front of the room with his/her back to the group.

2. The teacher chooses another child by pointing to that particular child. He/she tiptoes to the back of the chair and sings "Do you know the Muffin Man?" (Disguising his/her voice makes the task more difficult.)

3. The child sitting in the chair then sings, "Oh, yes, I know the Muffin Man, the Muffin Man. Oh, yes, I know the Muffin Man, who lives in Drury Lane."

4. The child has three chances to guess the Muffin Man. If correct, the Muffin Man may sit in the chair and another Muffin Man is chosen.

INSIDE AND OUTSIDE

Objective

To match pictures of objects that you can hear outside the house or you might hear inside the house

Materials

1. Pictures of objects you might hear inside the house and objects you hear outside the house.

2. Bristol board

3. Marking pens

4. Clear plastic adhesive

Making the Game

1. Rule the paper into three-inch squares and paste pictures on the squares. Cover with plastic, and cut apart.

2. Fold another piece of bristol into two parts — label one half "inside the house," and the other half "outside the house." Cover with plastic.

Playing the Game

1. Take out the small cards and help the child name the pictures.

2. Look at the two headings on the paper — "inside" and "outside." Help the child decide which pictures belong on the inside side and which belong on the outside side.

3. List all the sounds heard in the classroom or in the house, then all the sounds heard outside the school or house.

LOUD AND SOFT

Objective

To match pictures with loud and soft sounds

Materials

1. Pictures of objects that make sounds, such as: car, truck, leaf, baby, butterfly, train, feather, whistle, cat, kitten, mouse, piano, and telephone

2. Bristol board

3. Marking pens

4. Clear plastic adhesive

Making the Game

1. Rule the paper into three-inch squares and paste the pictures onto the cards. Cover with the plastic and cut apart.

2. Fold a large piece of bristol into two parts. Label one half "soft" and the other half "loud." Cover with the plastic.

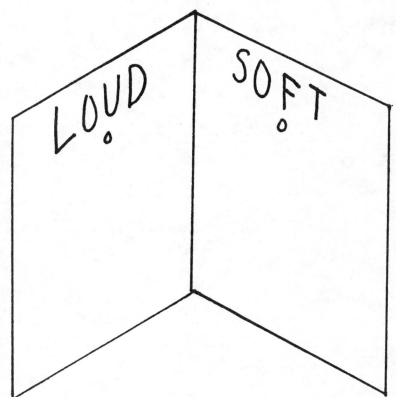

Playing the Game

1. Take out the small cards and discuss them with the child.

2. Look at the two headings on the paper — "loud" and "soft." Help the child decide which pictures belong on the soft side and which pictures belong on the loud side.

3. Find other pictures in old magazines that make a soft or loud sound. These may be pasted on sheets of paper labeled "soft" or "loud."

4. Find objects in the classroom or at home that make a loud sound and objects that make a soft sound.

Auditory Memory

DESCRIPTION LOTTO

Objective

To develop non–sequential auditory memory

Materials

1. Folding bristol
2. Assortment of pictures, two of each
3. Ruler, marking pens, paper cutter
4. Clear adhesive plastic

Making the Game

1. Rule the lotto cards 6" x 9". Rule each card into nine sections 3" x 3". Place a picture in each square. No two cards should have the same picture.
2. The stimulus cards will be 3" x 3". Put matching pictures on the cards.
3. Cover the lotto cards and the stimulus cards with plastic. Cut the stimulus cards apart with the paper cutter.

Playing the Game

1. Shuffle the deck of cards and place it face down in the middle of the playing area. Give each player a lotto card. Each player in turn will draw the top card from the deck. He describes the picture by naming the use of the item, or the shape, using any characteristics he chooses, but he may not name it. Each player claims cards by asking, "Is it . . .?" When a player successfully claims a card, the next player in turn describes the next card.
2. Your lotto cards may have a variety of pictures.

FIND THE SOUND

Objective

To develop non–sequential auditory memory

Materials

1. Bristol board, 12" x 18"

2. Folding bristol, 12" x 18"

3. Assortment of pictures, two of each

4. Cassette recorder

Making the Game

1. You will choose common environmental sounds to record (a bell, water faucet, car engine, dog barking, laughing, etc.). Record each sound for five seconds, pause for three seconds, repeat the sound for five seconds, pause for twelve seconds; follow this sequence with each sound. Record twelve distinct sounds.

2. Rule the bristol board into sections 4" x 4½". Rule the folding bristol into identical sections. Place matching pictures that identify your sounds on the board and the cards. Make very sure that your pictures clearly illustrate the sounds you have recorded.

3. Cover the pictures with clear plastic and cut the pictures on the folding bristol into cards.

Playing the Game

1. Name all the pictures with the child so that he/she has the necessary entry behavior to play the game without frustration.

2. Using earphones and a cassette playback, instruct the child to listen to the sound, select the card that illustrates the sound and place it on the matching picture on the gameboard.

3. For a group activity, make a set of cards and a gameboard for each player.

4. For a higher level activity, use similar but not identical pictures for the cards and the gameboard.

PICTURE FIND

Objective

To develop auditory memory

Materials

1. Folding bristol

2. File cards, 5" x 7"

3. Old nursery rhyme books

4. Assortment of related pictures

5. Clear adhesive plastic

Making the Game

1. Write your favorite nursery rhymes on the file cards, one to a card.

2. Rule the bristol into 4½" x 6", or 6" x 9" sections. In each section place a picture that corresponds to one of your rhymes.

3. Cover pictures and rhyme cards with plastic.

Playing the Game

1. Place pictures from four different nursery rhymes in front of the child. Name each picture with the child to make sure he has the necessary vocabulary to play the game.

2. Read one of the four rhymes to the child. Have the child point or name the picture that relates to the rhyme.

3. For a higher level activity, read the rhyme first, then place the pictures in front of the child and have him/her point out the correct picture.

"HEAR, HEAR"

Objective

To develop skill in memorizing in sequence

Materials

1. Folding bristol
2. Assortment of pictures, two each
3. Clear adhesive plastic

Making the Game

1. Rule the paper into 3" x 4" cards. Make two identical sets of cards with the pictures.
2. Cover the cards with plastic before you cut them apart.

Playing the Game

1. Teacher has a set of cards, the second set is spread out face up so that every member of the group can see all cards.
2. Teacher chooses three cards, names them, and places them face down. The first player selects the cards he/she has heard and places them in order. Teacher turns over his/her cards to check and see if the player is correct.
3. Higher level of activity would depend on the number of cards named and the length of time between each item named. For example, a three-second pause between naming five items would require a high degree of ability.

DO AS I DO

Objective

To develop sequential auditory memory

Materials

None

Making the Game

None

Playing the Game

1. The teacher claps or taps out a short rhythmic pattern. The first player repeats the pattern. Children in turn repeat a pattern created by the teacher.

2. For variety, have several rhythm instruments out. Teacher plays a rhythmic pattern on one of the instruments. The player may repeat the pattern with the same instrument or he/she may choose a different one.

Naming

COLOR LOTTO

Objective

To name colors

Materials

1. Folding bristol
2. Assorted pictures with one color
3. Marking pens
4. Ruler
5. Clear adhesive plastic

Making the Game

1. Decide on the colors you wish the class to name.
2. Rule the bingo cards 6" x 12". Divide each card into two rows of four spaces each. Each space will be 3" x 3".
3. The stimulus cards will be 3" x 3".
4. The top row of the bingo card may repeat a color that is in the bottom row.
5. The pictures will repeat the colors on different objects. The stimulus cards will have the identical pictures.
6. Cover the cards and the stimulus cards with plastic.

Playing the Game

1. The teacher will shuffle the stimulus cards. Give each player a bingo card. The teacher names the color and the object. The player who has the match claims the card. The first player to collect all the cards in a row is the winner.
2. For a higher skill activity, name the color and the object but do not show it to the group.

SHAPE BINGO

Objective

To name the shapes

Materials

1. Folding bristol

2. Marking pens

3. Ruler

4. Clear adhesive plastic

Making the Game

1. Decide on the shapes you wish the class to name.

2. Rule the bingo cards 6" x 12". Divide each card into two rows of four spaces each (3" x 3").

3. Draw your shapes in each section. The top row may have some of the shapes that are in the bottom row of each card, but be careful not to make any two cards that match.

4. Use different colors for your shapes, coloring some and outlining others.

5. The stimulus cards should have black shapes on white paper.

6. Cover the bingo cards and the stimulus cards with plastic.

Playing the Game

1. The teacher will shuffle the stimulus cards. Give each player a bingo card. The teacher names the card and shows it to the group. The players who have a match cover it with a marker. The first player to get one row covered is the winner.

2. For a higher skill activity, name the shape but do not show it to the group.

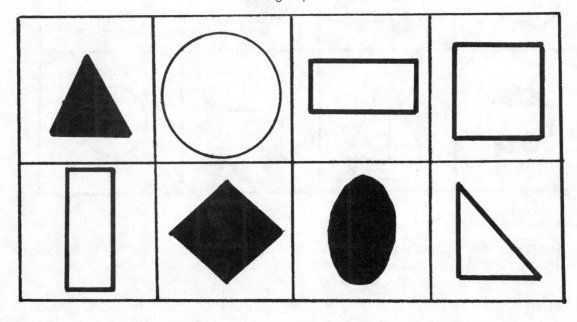

WHAT FRUIT IS IT?

Objective

To name different fruits

Materials

1. Folding bristol
2. Assorted pictures of fruit
3. Foam cube
4. Marking pens
5. Clear adhesive plastic
6. Ruler

Making the Game

1. Make a gameboard following the illustration.

2. Place the fruit pictures on the squares of the gameboard path. Cover the gameboard with plastic.

3. Place the numbers or sets of dots one to four on the die.

Playing the Game

1. Discuss the names of the fruits on the gameboard.

2. Place the gameboard in the center of the playing area.

3. Each player in turn will roll the die. He/she will move his/her marker the number of spaces indicated. If he/she can name the fruit, he/she remains there. If he/she cannot, he/she must move back. The first player to reach the end is the winner.

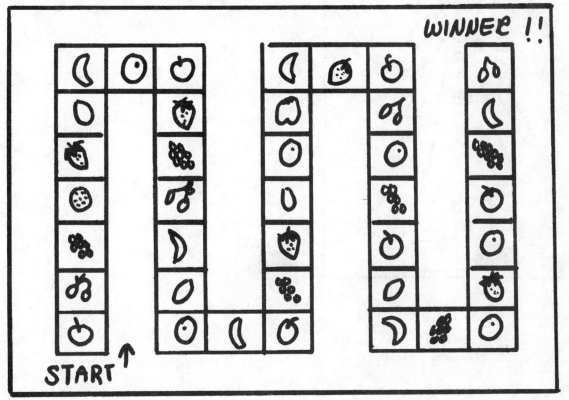

BOO HOO, I LOST MY . . .

Objective

To name body parts

Materials

1. Folding bristol

2. People pictures from magazines

3. Scissors

4. Clear adhesive plastic

Making the Game

1. From each people picture cut out a hand, an arm, a foot, etc. Cut out only one body part. Mount the rest of the picture on the folding bristol. Cover with plastic.

2. Mount the body parts that have been cut out on folding bristol. Cover with plastic. Cut the bristol close to the body part.

Playing the Game

1. Lay all the cards out before the group. Talk about each card in turn and name the missing body part.

2. Spread out the small body part cards and have the group place them on the appropriate people card.

BODY BINGO

Objective

To name body parts

Materials

1. Folding bristol

2. Assorted people pictures

3. Marking pens

4. Clear adhesive plastic

Making the Game

1. Decide upon the body parts you want the class to name.

2. Rule the bingo cards 6" x 9". Divide each card into nine sections, 2" x 3". Rule the stimulus cards 2" x 3".

3. Cut out the body parts you need from the assorted people pictures. You may also draw the body parts, or use a combination of hand drawings and pictures. Keep in mind that no picture should be larger than 2" x 3".

4. No two bingo cards should have the identical picture, but they may have the same body part.

5. Cover the bingo cards and the stimulus cards with plastic.

Playing the Game

1. The teacher shuffles the deck of stimulus cards. Each player has a bingo card. The teacher names the card and shows it to the group. The players who have a match cover it with a marker. The first player to get three spaces — diagonally, horizontally, or vertically — in a row is the winner.

2. For a higher skill activity, name the picture but do not show it to the group.

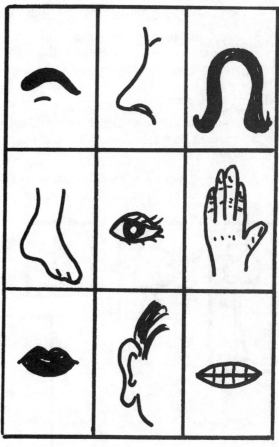

SIZE PUZZLE

Objective

To name sizes

Materials

1. Bristol board, 18" x 24"
2. Folding bristol
3. Assorted pictures that illustrate size
4. Marking pens
5. Clear adhesive plastic
6. Drapery hooks

Making the Game

1. Decide on the size-concept cards you wish to teach (example: tall–short, big–little, fat–thin, long–short, large–small).

2. Divide the bristol board into three sections, 8" x 18". Write the terms that indicate largeness on the left section using one color, the term "average" or "medium" in the middle section, and the terms that indicate smallness on the right section, using a different color. Cover the board with plastic. Insert a drapery hook at the top of each section.

3. Place the pictures on paper. The size will vary according to your picture. Color-code the back of the picture to match the color of the matching section on the bristol board. Cover with plastic. Make several sets of each size; including medium.

Playing the Game

1. Each size set will have three members (example: large, medium, small). Work with one size concept pair at a session. Have the group discuss where each member of the set belongs and why.

2. After all your size concept pairs have been introduced, allow the children to sort the sizes as an independent activity, using the color-coding as a check.

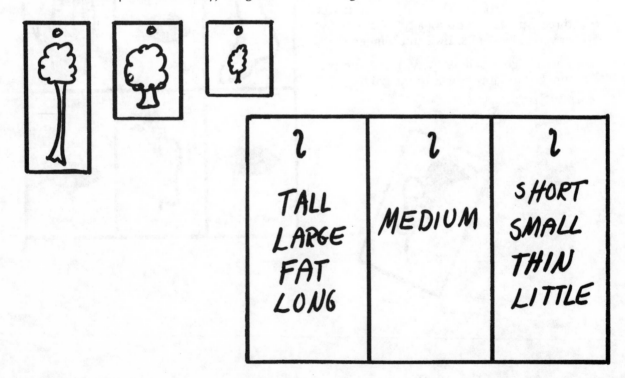

SOFT, HARD, ROUGH, SMOOTH

Objective

    To name the textures

Materials

1. Folding bristol

2. Assortment of materials, objects, pictures that illustrate texture

3. Clear adhesive plastic

Making the Game

1. Decide on the texture term you wish to teach.

2. Label 9" x 12" pieces of bristol with the texture. Cover with plastic and attach an object with that texture to the top of the card with staples or glue.

3. Mount pictures on 4" x 4" bristol and cover with plastic.

Playing the Game

1. Spread out the labeled sorting cards. Have the group decide where to place each item and picture.

2. Place an object in a box. Have the player describe how it feels. Take it out and see if the group agrees.

OPPOSITE DOMINOES

Objective

To differentiate basic opposite concepts

Materials

1. Folding bristol
2. Assortment of pictures
3. Marking pens
4. Clear adhesive plastic

Making the Game

1. Decide on the opposite concepts you wish to teach (example: hot-cold, young-old, up-down, inside-outside, wet-dry, big-little, open-closed, etc.).

2. Rule the dominoe cards 2¼" x 4". Divide the cards in half. Place the pictures on the cards, making sure that you place one concept on the left half of one card and the opposite concept match on the right half of a different card. Cover the cards with plastic.

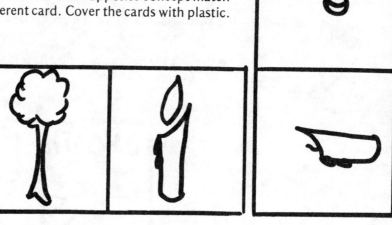

Playing the Game

1. Place the deck of cards face down in the middle of the playing area. Turn the top card over. Discuss the concepts on the card. Each player in turn draws cards until he draws one that matches the concept that is on the face-up card. The winner will be the player who makes the last match.

2. As children become more familiar with the concepts, you may put this game out as an independent activity.

WHAT AM I DOING?

Objective

To name action words, verbs

Materials

1. Folding bristol
2. Assorted pictures illustrating actions
3. Marking pens
4. Clear adhesive plastic

Making the Game

Rule the cards 3" x 3". Put the pictures on the cards and cover with plastic.

Playing the Game

1. Each child will draw a card in turn. He shows it to the teacher who explains it if necessary.
2. The group tries to guess the action being pantomimed by the player.

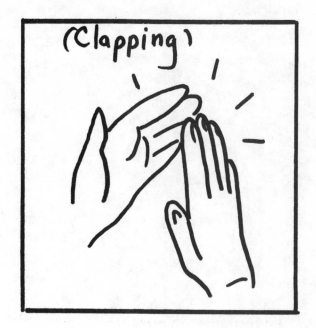

Rhyming

LACE A RHYME

Objective

To develop the skill of rhyming

Materials

1. Bristol board
2. Assorted pictures, rhyming pairs
3. Hole puncher
4. Shoelaces

Making the Game

1. Cut the bristol to a 9" x 12" rectangle.
2. You will have two rows of pictures; one down the left side of the gameboard and one down the right side. Place the rhyming pairs opposite each other on the board, but not in the same order.
3. Cover the board with plastic and punch holes next to each picture.
4. Thread a lace through each of the holes on the left side of the board. Knot the laces in back and in front of the holes to hold them in place.

Playing the Game

1. Name all the pictures on the board with the player.
2. Have the player match the pictures that rhyme by connecting the pictures on the left and the pictures on the right with the shoelace.

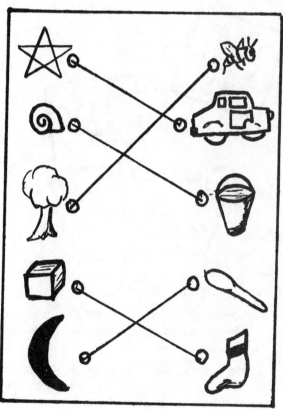

RHYMING SQUARES

Objective

To develop the skill of rhyming

Materials

1. Folding bristol
2. Assortment of pictures, rhyming sets of three or four
3. Assortment of small objects that rhyme with pictures
4. Clear adhesive plastic
5. Paper cutter

Making the Game

1. Rule the paper into 3" x 3" squares. Place rhyming pictures on the cards.
2. Cover the cards with plastic and cut apart with a paper cutter.

Playing the Game

1. Spread all the pictures and objects out on the playing area. The teacher chooses a picture or object and the group searches for all the pictures and objects that rhyme. Do this with all the rhyming sets.

2. Play "scramble" when the children have become familiar with the game. Give each player a different rhyming set to find. At a signal, have all the players search for their rhyming set at the same time. The first player to find all his cards and objects is the winner.

RHYMING LOTTO

Objective

To develop the skill of rhyming

Materials

1. Folding bristol
2. Assortment of pictures, rhyming pairs
3. Marking pens
4. Clear adhesive plastic
5. Ruler
6. Paper cutter

Making the Game

1. Rule the lotto cards 6" x 9", and divide them into nine sections, 2" x 3". Rule the stimulus cards 2" x 3".

2. Place one picture of the rhyming pair on the lotto card, and the other on a stimulus card.

3. Cover the lotto cards and the stimulus cards with plastic; cut the stimulus cards apart with a paper cutter.

Playing the Game

1. Shuffle the deck of cards and place it face down in the middle of the table. Give each player a lotto card. Have each player name the pictures of the card to check that he/she has the proper entry behavior to be successful in the game. Each player in turn will draw the top card and name it. The player who has the matching rhyming picture on his/her card will claim the picture. The winner is the first player to cover all his/her lotto pictures with the matching rhyming picture.

2. "Rhyming Bingo" can be played with this game using chips or markers. One player is the "caller." He/she alone names the cards. The player who has the matching rhyme covers it with a chip. The first player who has a diagonal, horizontal, or vertical row of three pictures covered is the winner, and says "bingo!"

RHYMING PUZZLES

Objective

To be able to match pictures of rhyming words

Materials

1. Folding bristol
2. Assortment of pictures, rhyming pairs
3. Scissors
4. Clear adhesive plastic
5. Paper cutter

Making the Game

1. Rule the paper into 3'' x 6'' sections.
2. Put pictures of rhyming pairs into the sections; one at the top and one at the bottom.
3. Cover the game with plastic.
4. Separate each section with the paper cutter.
5. Divide each section in half using a different puzzle cut for each matching pair.

Playing the Game

1. Lay all the top halves face up side by side. Lay all the bottom halves out side by side.
2. The player takes one half of a puzzle and finds the rhyming match. The puzzle will fit together if the correct match is made.
3. To add a degree of difficulty, lay the top and bottom puzzle pieces out randomly.

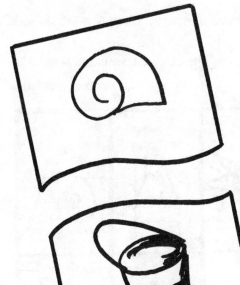

RHYMING CHIP CONCENTRATION

Objective

To be able to match pictures that rhyme; to reinforce visual memory

Materials

1. Twenty-four poker chips
2. Folding bristol
3. Assortment of pictures, rhyming pairs
4. Marking pen
5. Clear adhesive plastic

Making the Game

1. Draw twenty-four circles on the paper using a poker chip to trace around.
2. Choose twelve pairs of rhyming pictures, cutting them to fit into the circles if necessary and place them randomly in the circles. Cover the game with plastic.
3. Store the chips in a small container.

Playing the Game

1. This activity works well for one or two players.
2. Cover all the circles with the poker chips. The player uncovers two pictures. If they rhyme, he/she keeps the chips. If the pictures do not rhyme, he/she replaces the chips. The player continues his/her turn as long as he/she makes matches. The player loses his/her turn when he/she uncovers two pictures that do not rhyme. The player at the end of the game with the most chips is the winner.

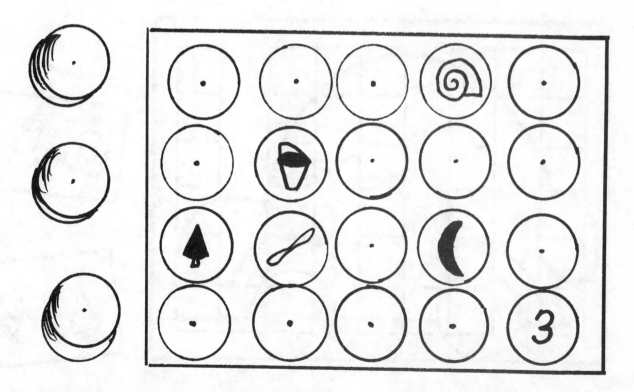

DOES IT RHYME?

Objective

To be able to discriminate between words that rhyme and words that do not rhyme

Materials

1. Bristol board
2. Folding bristol
3. Assortment of pictures, some rhyming pairs
4. Ruler
5. Clear adhesive plastic
6. Marking pens
7. Paper cutter

Making the Game

1. Following the illustration for your gameboard, copy it onto the bristol board. On a 12" x 18" gameboard, the spaces should be approximately 1½" x 2". You may decorate the board by drawing the outline of a train, animal, flower, etc.

2. Rule the cards 3" x 5" on the folding bristol. You should have at least twenty cards in the deck. On fifteen cards you will place two pictures that rhyme; on the remaining five you will place two pictures that do not rhyme.

3. Cover the cards and gameboard with plastic, and cut the cards apart with the paper cutter.

Playing the Game

1. Place the deck of cards face down. The first player draws the top card and names the pictures. If the two pictures rhyme, he/she moves his/her marker three spaces. If the two pictures do not rhyme, he/she moves the marker only one space. The winner is the first player to reach the end.

2. This gameboard may be used with any number of games you may make.

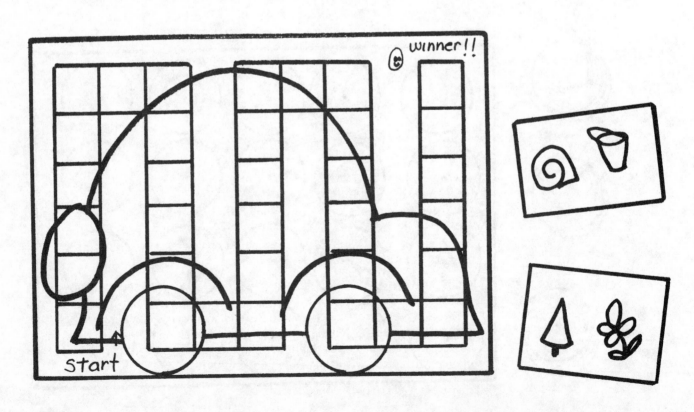

RHYMING CONCENTRATION

Objective

   To reinforce the skill of rhyming

Materials

1. Folding bristol
2. Assortment of pictures, rhyming pairs
3. Clear adhesive plastic
4. Ruler
5. Paper cutter

Making the Game

1. Rule the cards into 3" x 3" squares. Place a picture in each square. You will want to begin with twelve rhyming pairs.

2. Cover the cards with plastic before you cut them apart with the paper cutter.

Playing the Game

1. Put the cards face down in rows on the table. The first player turns over two cards. If they match, he/she keeps them and continues turning two cards over at a time until he/she cannot find a rhyming pair. The player then replaces the pair that does not rhyme in their original spot. Each player tries to recall where each card is, in order to help match rhyming pairs. The player with the most rhyming pairs is the winner.

2. "Rhyming Old Maid" can be played with this set of cards. Deal out all the cards, one at a time, to the players in turn. One card will not have a rhyming match. It will be the "old maid." The first player draws one card from the hand of the player to his/her left. If the card is a rhyming match, he/she lays down the pair. The player names the rhyme. Each player in turn draws a card from another's hand. A player who runs out of cards drops out of the game. The player who is left with the "old maid" is the loser.

THE RHYMING CHASE

Objective

To provide a rhyme for a given word

Materials

1. Folding bristol
2. Assortment of pictures, some duplicates
3. Ruler
4. Clear adhesive plastic
5. Marking pens
6. Paper cutter

Making the Game

1. Follow the illustration for your gameboard path. On a 12" x 18" gameboard, the spaces should be approximately 1½" x 2". Place four pictures randomly in spaces; one near the end, one near the beginning, two in between.

2. Rule the cards 2" x 3". Place pictures on the cards that will be easy for the child to rhyme (example: car, ball, bell, bee, hat, etc.). On eight of the cards you will repeat the pictures you placed on the gameboard (twice). Under each rhyming picture place the number 1, 2, 3, or 4. Do not place a number on the cards that have the same pictures as the gameboard. (Confused? Trust us.)

3. Cover the gameboard and the cards with plastic; cut the cards apart with a paper cutter.

Playing the Game

1. Place the deck of cards face down. The first player turns over the top card. He/she names the picture and then says a word that rhymes with the picture. If he/she is correct, he/she moves the number of spaces on the board indicated by the number on the card.

2. If the player turns over a card that has one of the gameboard pictures on it, he/she moves backward or forward to that space. These cards add a little variety to the game.

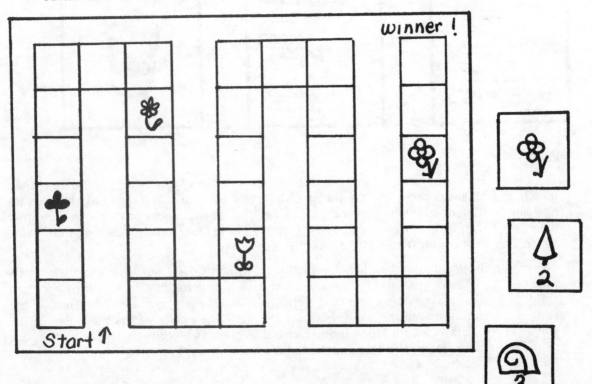

Alphabet

ALPHABET LACING

Objective

To lace the outline of a picture in alphabetical order

Materials

1. Colorful pictures from coloring books, workbooks, stickers, etc., that are large and simple in design

2. Tagboard or cardboard

3. Clear plastic adhesive

4. Hole punch

5. Shoelace

Making the Game

1. Mount the picture on the tagboard. Around the outline of the picture, write the alphabet. Depending upon how difficult you wish to make the game, you may use the whole alphabet or just part of it.

2. Cover the card with plastic, front and back.

3. Punch holes next to each letter.

Playing the Game

1. The child takes the sewing card and a shoelace.

2. He/she finds the letter "A." The child then proceeds to sew, going in and out of the holes in alphabetical order. If help is needed, the child may refer to an alphabet chart.

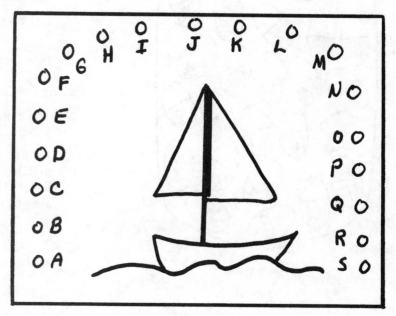

THE CANDY GAME

Objective

To match capital letters with their lower case letters

Materials

1. Large piece of tagboard or cardboard
2. Marking pens
3. Wallpaper
4. Clear plastic adhesive

Making the Game

1. On the large piece of tagboard, draw a large jar. Cut it out.

2. Cut out twenty-six jellybeans from various patterns of wallpaper. These should be oval-shaped.

3. On the upper half of each jellybean, print the capital letter; on the bottom half, print the lower case letter.

4. Cut each jellybean in half. Paste the upper halves in the jar, in alphabetical order.

5. Cover with clear plastic, if desired.

Playing the Game

1. The child spreads the bottom halves of the jellybeans in front of him/her.

2. He/she then matches the jellybeans by matching the lower case letter to the capital letter. The pattern will match if the letters are placed correctly.

MATCH THE ALPHABET

Objective

To match uppercase letters with their lower case letters

Materials

1. Colored tagboard or heavy oaktag
2. Marking pens
3. Clear plastic adhesive
4. Scissors

Making the Game

1. Section the board into 5" x 3" rectangles. On the top half write the upper case letter; on the bottom half, write the lower case letter.

2. Cover with clear plastic and cut the cards out. Cut each letter with a curved line. Make no two sets of curved lines alike.

Playing the Game

1. Take the set of upper case letters and spread them out in even rows.

2. Have the child match the lower case letters to the upper case letters. If the choice is not correct, the letters will not fit.

WALDO THE WORM

Objective

To match capital letters with their lower case letters

Materials

1. A large piece of tagboard or cardboard; another piece of tagboard for small pieces

2. Marking pens

3. Scissors

4. Clear plastic adhesive

Making the Game

1. Draw a large wiggly worm on the large piece of tagboard.

2. Divide the worm into twenty–six segments.

3. Write a capital letter in each segment from A to Z.

4. Cut twenty–six small, individual segments to match the segments on the worm.

5. Write a lower case letter on each small segment, a to z.

6. Cover with clear adhesive plastic.

Playing the Game

1. The child spreads the small segments in front of him/her.

2. He/she then matches all the letters of the alphabet on the worm from a to z.

3. The child will say each letter as he/she places it on the match.

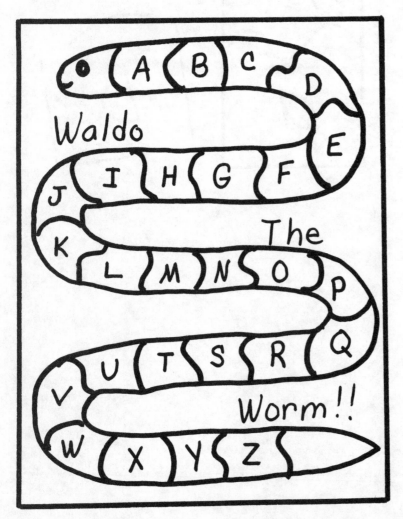

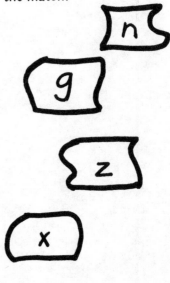

CHIP CONCENTRATION

Objective

To identify and match letters of the alphabet

Materials

1. Tagboard or bristol board
2. Marking pen
3. Poker chips or circle discs
4. Clear plastic adhesive

Making the Game

1. Make an even number of circles (the same size as the poker chips) all over the large-sized board.
2. In each circle make a letter. Two circles should have the same letter.
3. Smile faces can be put into some of the circles.
4. Cover the board with clear adhesive.

Playing the Game

1. Two or more players can play. All circles are covered by the chips.
2. The first player turns over two chips. If the letters match, he/she may keep the chips and take another turn. If the letters do not match, they must be covered and the next player may proceed.
3. The game proceeds until all chips have been won, because the players have found the matching letters.
4. The player who has the most chips in his/her possession is the winner.

ALPHABET DOMINOES

Objective

To match identical letters

Materials

1. Bristol board or oaktag
2. Marking pens
3. Scissors
4. Clear adhesive plastic

Making the Game

1. Section the bristol board into 4" x 2" rectangles. The rectangles should be divided every 2" by a line.
2. Letters of the alphabet are marked in each side of the rectangle. They may be all capitals, all lower case letters, or mixed.
3. The cards should be covered with plastic and then cut.

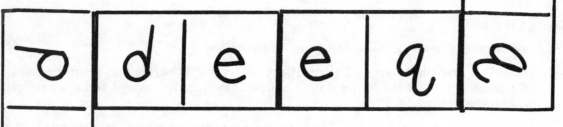

Playing the Game

1. One or two players may participate.
2. All cards are placed face down in a pile. One card face up is placed in the middle of the table.
3. One player draws a card from the pile. If he/she can match the card on the table, the card may be placed down and another card is drawn. If the card cannot be placed, he/she keeps the card until it can be used when it is the player's turn again.
4. The next player takes a turn and the play is continued until one player does not have any more cards and there are no cards on the table.
5. All cards that are matched must match the touching card on all sides.

STEPPING STONES

Objective

To identify and name the letters of the alphabet

Materials

1. Bristol board
2. Marking pens
3. Scissors
4. Clear adhesive plastic

Making the Game

1. Cut the bristol board in oval shapes.
2. Print any letters of the alphabet. They may be all lower case, all upper case, or mixed.
3. Cover the letters with clear plastic.

Playing the Game

1. The child will place the stepping stones on the floor, one at a time.
2. He/she will name each stone's letter as he/she steps on it.
3. If the child does not say the correct name, tell him/her the name of the letter. He/she then goes back to the beginning and names them all again. If a small group of children wish to play, they must take turns. The first one to reach the end and name all the letters correctly is the winner.

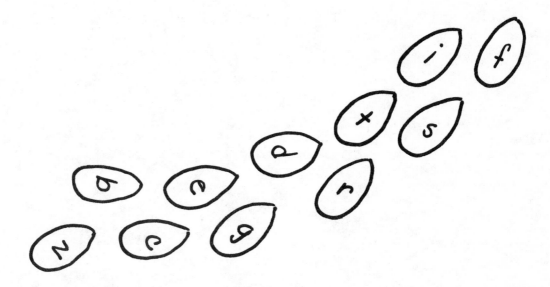

Phonics

LACE THE SOUND

Objective

To match a consonant letter with a picture that has its corresponding beginning sound

Materials

1. Bristol board or oaktag
2. Marking pens
3. Stickers or small pictures from old workbooks
4. Clear plastic adhesive
5. Shoelaces
6. Hole punch

Making the Game

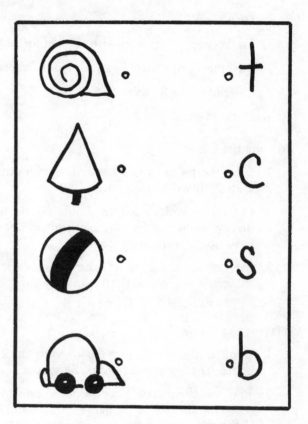

1. On the right–hand side of the board, vertically print consonant letters.

2. On the left–hand side, paste pictures opposite the letters but not in order of the letters; however, the pictures must correspond with the beginning sounds of the letters printed.

3. Punch holes next to each letter on the left; the holes should also be made next to the pictures on the right. Cover with plastic.

4. Next to the letter, knot a shoelace in each hole (the knot should be in the back).

Playing the Game

1. The child will say the sound of the letter on the left. He/she then finds a picture that begins with that letter sound.

2. He/she takes the shoelace next to the letter and places it in the hole next to the picture selected.

3. Proceed until all shoelaces have matched all the pictures.

PUZZLE GAME

Objective

To identify the beginning sound in a word and match the sound with its letter name

Materials

1. Stickers or workbooks with large colorful pictures
2. Two pieces of bristol board or tagboard (colored), 12" x 18"
3. Clear plastic adhesive
4. Marking pens

Making the Game

1. Glue the pictures you have chosen on one 12" x 18" piece of board. Ten pictures, well separated, fit well. Cover with plastic.

2. Cut out the pictures into simple puzzle shapes, using curves and straight lines. Each puzzle piece should contain one picture. Do not cut any pictures in half. Each puzzle piece should have one picture in the center.

3. Starting with the top left corner, trace the puzzle pieces on the second piece of board. Print the beginning sound (letter) in the center of each outlined puzzle shape on the second board. Cover with plastic contact paper.

Playing the Game

1. Look at the puzzle gameboard with the child. Help him/her to identify the letters on the board. Discuss the shapes of the spaces.

2. Take out the puzzle pieces. Choose one and have the child name it; then he/she finds a space that contains the letter naming the sound he/she hears at the beginning of the picture word. If the puzzle piece fits, it is correct. Continue until all pieces of the puzzle fit.

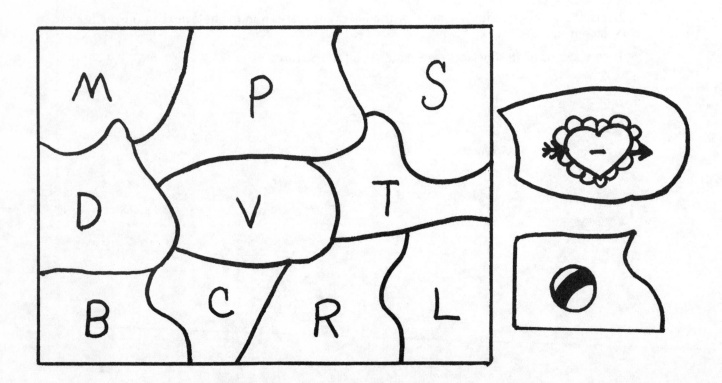

PICK AND CHECK

Objective

To select pictures that begin with the key letter sound on the strip

Materials

1. Bristol board or oaktag
2. Marking pens
3. Stickers or workbook pictures
4. Hole punch
5. Clear plastic adhesive

Making the Game

1. Cut the bristol board into an 18" x 14" strip.

2. Place a key letter sound with a picture beginning with that sound on the top of the strip.

3. Place pictures down the left side of the strip, making sure there are some pictures that begin with the key letter.

4. On the right side of the pictures, punch a hole next to each picture.

5. On the back side, color-code the outline of the punched hole if it matches the sound of the key picture and letter.

6. Cover the strips with clear plastic, punching out the holes again.

Playing the Game

1. The child will identify the letter by saying its sound.

2. The child then names all the pictures on the strip.

3. He/she will select the pictures that begin with the key letter sound at the top of the strip. He/she will put a pencil through the holes next to the picture selected.

4. Check the back of the strip. Correct selections are color-coded.

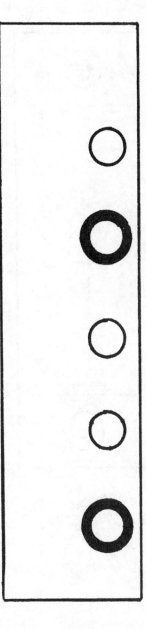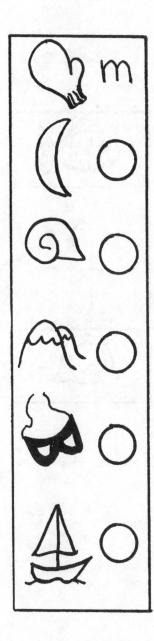

TAKE A PEEK

Objective

To select a picture that begins with the key letter sound

Materials

1. Colored bristol board or oaktag
2. Marking pens
3. Stickers or pictures from workbooks
4. Clear plastic adhesive

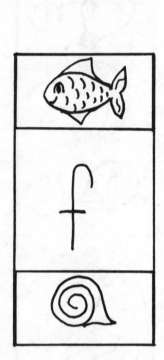

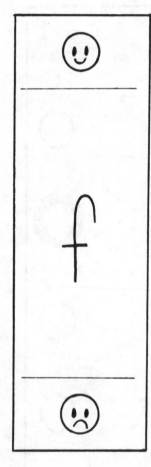

Making the Game

1. Cut 12" x 4½" strips from the bristol board.
2. Fold down 2" from both ends of the strip.
3. Write a letter in the middle of the strip.
4. Paste pictures on both ends of the folds, one beginning with the letter sound in the middle of the strip (if desired, ending sounds or middle sounds may be the objective).
5. Make a "smile" face under the correct picture, an unhappy face under the incorrect answer.
6. Cover with clear plastic.

Playing the Game

1. The child says the letter name and the sound for the letter in the middle of the strip.
2. He/she says the names of the pictures, then decides which picture begins with the letter sound.
3. He/she lifts the picture fold. If correct, it will be a "smile" face.

SOUND CARD MATCH

Objective

To identify the beginning sound in a word with its letter name

Materials

1. Stickers or colorful workbook pictures

2. Two pieces of folding bristol or tagboard, 12" x 18"

3. Ruler

4. Waterbased felt marker

5. Clear plastic adhesive

Making the Game

1. Rule the paper into alternating rows of 1¾" x 3" and 1¼" x 3".

2. Place the picture in the 1¾" space and print the beginning sound in the 1¼" space. Cover with plastic and cut apart with a paper cutter. Print the beginning sound on the back of the picture card.

Playing the Game

1. First, take the picture cards and place them in neat rows, picture side up. Next, take the small letter cards and place them in rows, letter side up.

2. The child then takes a picture, names it, and selects a letter card he/she thinks names the beginning sound. He/she then turns the picture over. The letter on the back will match the letter chosen if correct.

3. Giving each picture its proper name is very important in this game. If the child needs help in naming the pictures, it should be given.

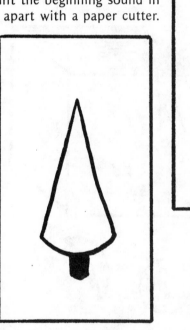

4. The game can be played with ending or medial sounds if designated and made for that purpose.

SOUND BOXES

Objective

To find concrete objects that begin with a designated sound

Materials

1. Small empty boxes

2. Construction paper or paint

3. Scissors and paste (optional)

4. Marking pens

Making the Game

1. Decorate the boxes with construction paper or paint. The children should help in the project.

2. Print the letter and make a picture or paste a picture that begins with the sound of this letter on the front of the box.

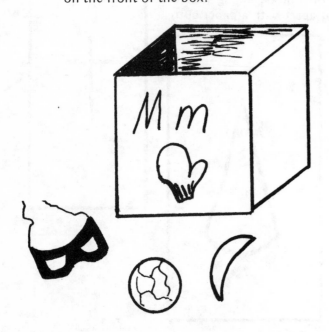

Playing the Game

1. The child will look at the letter and picture on the box, one at a time. He/she will say the sound of the letter.

2. He/she will look in the box of small concrete objects gathered around the classroom or the house and will find the object that begins with the sound (a pair of socks for /s/, a toy mouse for /m/).

3. A new box can be added as new sounds are taught.

YES OR NO

Objective

    To discriminate between beginning or ending sounds that match

Materials

1. Tagboard or bristol board

2. Stickers or small pictures from old workbooks

3. Marking pens

4. Clear plastic adhesive

Making the Game

1. Make a gameboard out of large-sized tagboard.

2. Make rectangle cards. Divide the cards in half. On both halves paste different pictures; some must begin or end with the same sound, others must be different.

3. Cover the gameboard and cards with clear plastic.

Playing the Game

1. Each player must have a marker. The first player chooses a card from the pile of cards with the pictures face down.

2. The player says the picture word. He/she decides if it begins or ends the same. If it does, the player may move his/her marker two spaces. If it does not, the player does not move.

3. Play continues with this procedure, each player taking his/her turn. The first to reach the end of the gameboard is the winner.

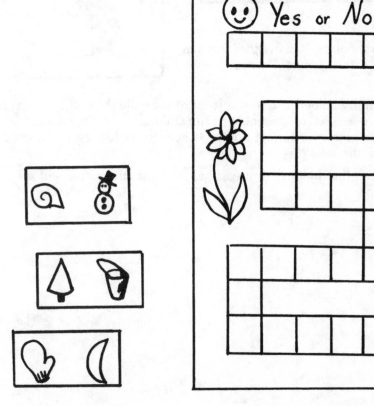

SOUND HOLDERS

Objective

To identify a beginning sound in a word with its letter name

Materials

1. Colorful workbook pictures or stickers
2. Colorful folding bristol or tagboard, 12" x 18"
3. Marking pens
4. Clear plastic adhesive
5. Paper cutter
6. Stapler

Making the Game

1. Rule the paper into 3" x 3" squares.

2. Place the pictures in the squares, cover with plastic and cut apart with a paper cutter.

3. For the holders, use tagboard cut to 4½" x 6". Fold up the bottom edge within 2" of the top. Write the capital and small letters at the top, and place a picture of something that begins with the letter next to them. Staple the sides.

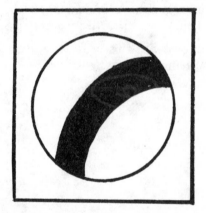

Playing the Game

1. Take the first holder. Remove the cards and name them with the child. Do this for each holder.

2. Place the empty holders in a row in front of the child. Mix all the cards and place them face down in a pile next to the holders. The child takes the top card, names the picture, and places it back into the correct holder. If help is needed, assist the child. All the rest of the cards follow the same procedure.

3. The child can find pictures in magazines and paste the pictures of the sounds on a separate piece of paper.

SOUND TURTLE

Objective

To identify and match beginning sounds by finding pictures that begin with the same sounds

Materials

1. Stickers or pictures
2. Bristol board or oaktag
3. Marking pens
4. Clear plastic adhesive

Making the Game

1. Cut the bristol board into the shape of a turtle approximately 6" x 8".
2. Cut small cards approximately 1½" x 2".
3. Draw or put a picture in the middle of the larger card. Draw four boxes in each corner, 1½" x 2".
4. Draw four different pictures beginning with the same sound as each illustrated large card.
5. Cover all the cards with clear adhesive plastic.

Playing the Game

1. The child looks at the center picture of each card and names it.
2. He/she then looks at a picture (small card) and names it. Then an illustrated large card with a picture that begins the same way is found. He/she places it in one of the boxes.
3. The child proceeds with all the other picture cards until the illustrated cards have four picture cards on each.

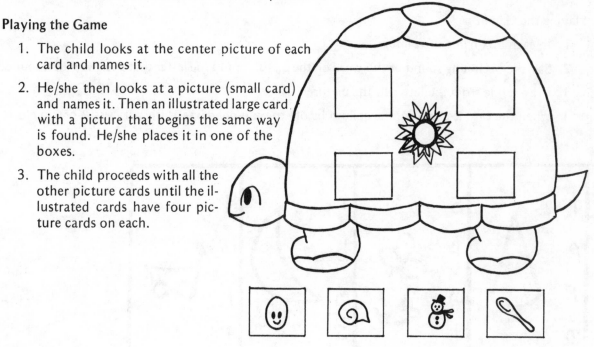

MAGIC SOUNDS

Objective

To discriminate beginning sounds of letters by drawing a line from a letter to the picture of a word that begins with the letter sound

Materials

1. Bristol board or oaktag

2. Marking pens

3. Stickers

4. Clear plastic adhesive

Making the Game

1. Cut the bristol board to size, approximately 8" x 10".

2. Divide the card into boxes.

3. In each box draw a picture. Print four letters at the left of the picture in each box. One of the letters must be the beginning sound of the picture.

4. Cover the card with clear plastic adhesive.

Playing the Game

1. In each box name the picture.

2. Say the beginning sound of the word on the picture. Find the letter that goes with that sound.

3. Draw a line from the letter to the picture.

4. When the card is checked, the child rubs off the crayoned lines with a dry tissue or soft cloth.

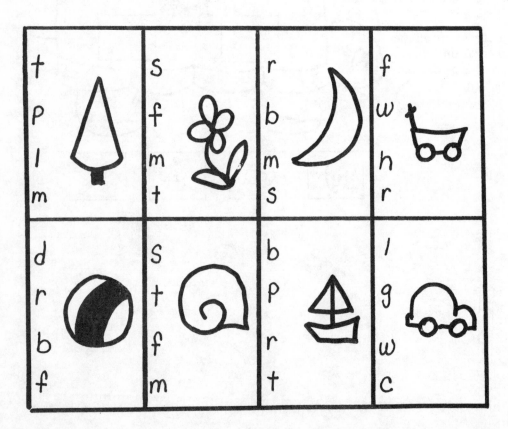

CIRCLE, CIRCLE

Objective

To circle pictures that begin with the designated letters

Materials

1. Bristol board or tagboard
2. Marking pens
3. Stickers or pictures from old workbooks
4. Clear plastic adhesive
5. Plastic circles from soda holders

Making the Game

1. On top of the bristol board print three letters.
2. Cut and paste pictures that begin with the sounds of the letters at the top over the rest of the surface.
3. Cover with clear plastic.
4. Cut apart the plastic carry holders of soda cans. These will be circular.

Playing the Game

1. Use one plastic circle to enclose a letter on the top of the board.
2. The child then finds pictures that begin with this letter sound.
3. He/she circles all the pictures that begin with this sound.
4. Another letter is then circled and the pictures corresponding to the beginning sound of this letter are then circled.
5. Again the circles are removed and the same procedure for the third letter is accomplished.

THE SOUND WHEEL

Objective

To identify beginning sounds of words by finding pictures that begin with the sound of a designated letter

Materials

1. Scissors
2. Magazines or stickers
3. Pizza board or cardboard
4. Paste
5. Marking pen
6. Clear plastic adhesive

Making the Game

1. Cut the cardboard into a large circle. Mark the circle into pie-shaped wedges.
2. Print a letter near the center of the circle of each wedge.
3. Paste stickers or cut pictures from magazines that begin with the sound of the letters in the pie on small cards.
4. Cover completely with clear plastic.

Playing the Game

1. The child looks at the small cards and names the pictures.
2. He/she finds the letter that begins the sound of the picture and places that picture in the wedge.

3. He/she proceeds until all the cards are used.

4. The child makes a duplicate pie or has one made for him/her. He/she then looks in an old magazine for pictures that have the same initial sounds. He/she cuts and pastes the pictures in the appropriate wedges.

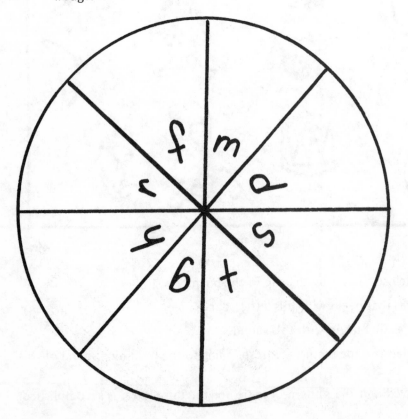

CLOTHESPIN GAME

Objective

> To match letters and pictures that have the same beginning sound (ending or middle sounds may also be used)

Materials

1. Pizza board or a circle made from tagboard
2. Marking pens
3. Stickers or pictures from workbooks
4. Clear plastic adhesive
5. Clothespins (the clip type)

Making the Game

1. Cut out the circle from tagboard (large).
2. Section off the pizza board into wedges.
3. Paste one picture in each pie–shaped wedge.
4. Cover the board with clear plastic.
5. Print one letter (the beginning sound of each picture) on each clothespin.

Playing the Game

1. The child names all the pictures on the pizza board.
2. He/she spreads out all the clothespins and says the sound of each letter, one at a time.
3. After saying the sound, he/she clips the clothespin on the edge of the wedge that has a picture with the same beginning sound.
4. Play continues until all clothespins are used and all wedges are covered.

TIC-TAC-TOE

Objective

To name the sounds of letters

Materials

1. Bristol board

2. Marking pen

3. Ruler

4. Clear adhesive plastic

Making the Game

1. Cut the bristol board into squares, 3" x 3".

2. Mark each square with a consonant letter.

3. On a 9" x 12" card, label the top "Tic," "Tac," "Toe."

4. Divide and mark the card into nine squares.

5. Cover the card and squares with clear plastic.

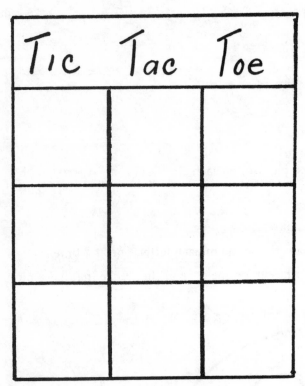

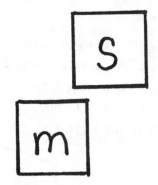

Playing the Game

1. Two players take turns choosing one card from the pile.

2. The player names the sound of the letter chosen.

3. If successful, he/she may make an "X" or "O" in a square selected.

4. The first player to complete a row with his/her selected symbol of "X" or "O" is the winner. The row may be horizontal, vertical, or diagonal.

SPIN A SOUND

Objective

To find a picture on a gameboard that begins with a letter sound

Materials

1. Tagboard or bristol board
2. Hole punch
3. Marking pens
4. Clear plastic adhesive
5. Stickers or pictures from old workbooks
6. Markers for playing the game
7. Paper fastener

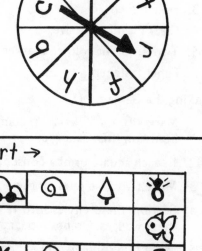

Making the Game

1. Make a gameboard from a large-size piece of tagboard. Rule off boxes on the zig-zag shape of the gameboard.

2. Paste a picture in each box. The pictures must begin (or end, if desired) with the letters on the spinner. An unhappy face may be added.

3. Make a spinner with approximately a 6" circumference. Divide the circle into pie-shaped wedges. In each wedge print a letter; it may be beginning or ending sounds, according to the objective of your game.

4. Cover the board and spinner board with clear plastic.

5. Make a spinner and fasten in the middle of the circle.

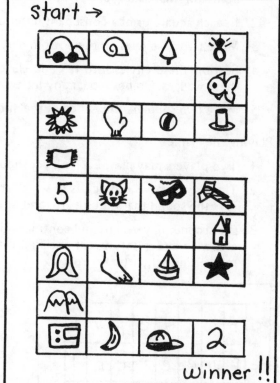

Playing the Game

1. The first player spins the spinner. He/she says the sound of the letter which the spinner is pointing to. He/she then places his/her marker on a picture that begins or ends with that sound.

2. The next player proceeds and the play continues until a player reaches WINNER!

3. An unhappy face may be put on the board at intervals. If a player spins an unhappy face, he/she loses his/her turn.

BLOCK IT

Objective

To match a consonant letter with its phonetic sound

Materials

1. 18" x 24" board of oaktag or bristol board
2. Marking pens
3. Hole punch
4. Clear plastic adhesive
5. Two different colored markers for the game (circles)
6. Paper fasteners

Making the Game

1. Mark off a 10" x 12" rectangle on the sheet of oaktag. Mark off approximately forty 1" boxes on this rectangle.

2. In each square print a consonant letter until all boxes are lettered.

3. Make two 5" circles on the bottom part of the board.

4. Section these circles into ten and eleven pie-shaped wedges. Print all consonant letters in these wedges. Do not repeat any letters. Cover the board with clear plastic.

5. Make two spinners and fasten in the middle of the circles.

Playing the Game

1. Two players may play. Each player should have different colored markers.

2. The players have a choice as to which spinner to spin. After making the choice, he/she spins, says the sound that it points to, and puts his/her marker on that letter.

3. The second player spins and continues the play in the same manner. If he/she wishes to block a row in order to prevent the first player from covering a row, he/she may place his/her marker in that particular row.

4. The first player to cover an entire row — across, up, or down — is the winner.

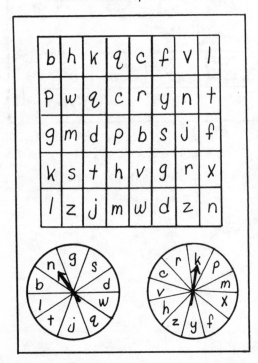

SOUND BOARD

Objective

To match a beginning sound of a picture with its letter name

Materials

1. Colored oaktag or bristol board
2. Stickers or old workbook pictures
3. Marking pens
4. Paper fasteners
5. Hole punch
6. Clear plastic adhesive
7. Markers to cover letters (beans, circles, etc.)

Making the Game

1. Cut a piece of oaktag into a 9" x 9" square. Then cut four pieces into rocket-shaped appendages. The appendages are approximately 9" x 4½" (stopping the rectangle at this point and ending the piece into a triangle; see diagram on page 94).
2. On the 9" x 9" square make an 8" circle and divide it into eight pie shapes.
3. On the pie shapes paste the stickers or pictures in each wedge. Each picture should start with a different sound.
4. Make a spinner and fasten it in the middle of the circle.
5. On the rocket-shaped appendages make rectangles approximately 5" x 4". Divide these into sixteen boxes. In each box write a letter representing the beginning sounds of the pictures. The four cards should have the same letters but in various orders.
6. Place the four pieces touching the sides of the 9" squares. Cover with clear plastic.

Playing the Game

1. Each player chooses a rocket-shaped board. Four players may play.
2. The first player spins the spinner. He/she must say the sound. All players may cover the beginning sound of that picture.
3. Each player takes a turn, continues to spin, says the sound, and covers the letter that represents that sound.
4. The first player to cover all letters in a row — across, up, down, or diagonally — is the winner.
5. Another variation: the player who spins is the only one to cover the letter when he/she says the sound.

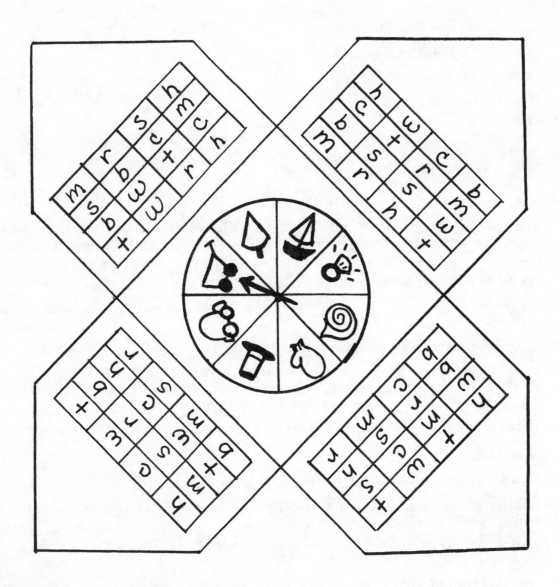

SNOWMAN GAME

Objective

To match ending patterns

Materials

1. Large-sized tagboard and bristol board
2. Paper fasteners
3. Marking pens
4. Clear plastic adhesive
5. Hole punch

Making the Game

1. Across the top of the large-sized tagboard make snowmen's faces with top hats.
2. Place paper fasteners under each face. Also place four or five paper fasteners evenly spaced in a row under each snowman.
3. Make as many circles that will fit in each row under the snowmen.
4. Make as many scarves that will fit under each snowman's chin.
5. Punch a hole in each scarf knot and at the top of each circle.
6. Print an ending pattern (at, in, un, it, etc.) on each scarf. Print four or five words using the ending patterns on the circles.
7. Cover all with clear plastic adhesive. Repunch when necessary.

Playing the Game

1. The child reads the ending patterns.
2. He/she sorts out the circles or snowballs and places them on the paper fastener under the matching ending pattern (example: cat, mat, hat, fat under the "at" family, etc.).
3. The child reads each word and continues until all snowballs are used.
4. The endings may be changed periodically.
5. For two or more players, each child chooses an ending scarf. The first player to build a snowman is the winner.

Classification

WHAT BELONGS?

Objective

To select a picture that is different from a row of pictures, and tell why

Materials

1. Bristol board
2. Scissors
3. Hole punch
4. Red marking pen plus other colors
5. Clear adhesive plastic
6. Pencil

Making the Game

1. Cut the bristol board approximately 3" x 12".

2. Draw a picture on a strip approximately 2½"; four pictures in all. Examples are: things to ride on, one will have no wheels (a sled); all are animals (tame), one is wild; all are wearing apparel for the feet, one is for the head.

3. Punch a hole under each picture.

4. Color–code the different categories on the back of the strip.

5. Cover with clear plastic. Punch out the covered hole.

FRONT

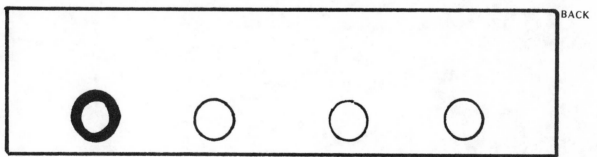

BACK

Playing the Game

1. The child looks at the card.

2. He/she tells what is the same about three of the pictures, and what is different about the one selected.

3. He/she will put a pencil in the hole under the picture that is different.

4. He/she will turn the card over to see if the hole was red-coded. If it is, he/she is correct.

COLOR SORT

Objective

To match colors

Materials

1. Oaktag or bristol board
2. Scissors
3. Colored marking pens
4. Containers for the color strips (juice cans or pockets on tagboard)

Making the Game

1. Cut the oaktag or bristol board into 1" x 4" strips.
2. Color-code each strip, at least six per color.
3. Color-code each container that receives the strips.
4. If a pocket chart is used, make the pockets and paste on a large piece of cardboard or oaktag.
5. For a more difficult skill, write color words instead of coded colors on the strips.

Playing the Game

1. The child sorts the strips.
2. The child puts a strip into its matching container.
3. The child continues until all strips are used.
4. The child names all the colors.

FEEL THE MATCH

Objective

    To match objects that are alike in texture

Materials

1. 6" circles made out of various materials (sandpaper, corduroy, velvet, leather, sponge rubber, fur remnants, etc.)
2. Scissors
3. A container for holding the circles
4. A blindfold

Making the Game

1. Cut out the 6" circles from the materials available. Cut two out of the same material.
2. Place the circles in a container.

Playing the Game

1. The child puts the blindfold on.
2. Spread the circles in front of the child.
3. He/she is to match the circles that feel the same.
4. After matching all the circles, the blindfold can be removed to check the matches.

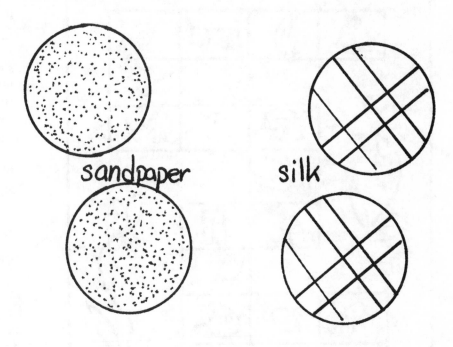

SPIN THE GROUP

Objective

To match categories of the same group on a gameboard

Materials

1. Cardboard gameboard

2. Stickers of various categories (fruits, animals, toys, etc.)

3. Marking pens

4. Spinner

5. Markers, one for each player

Making the Game

1. Make a spinner board of the various categories, at least one of each. An unhappy face can be one of the categories.

2. Make a gameboard, alternating the categories that were put on the spinner.

3. Cover the gameboard and spinner with clear plastic. Use a paper fastener or a "buttoneer" plastic button fastener to attach the pointer made from a piece of cardboard.

Playing the Game

1. Discuss the various categories on the spinner. The unhappy face means a loss of a turn.

2. Each player takes a turn, he/she spins the pointer and moves his/her marker to the first fruit if the pointer is on a fruit.

3. The game proceeds as each person takes their turn. The player who lands in the last space is the winner.

CLASSIFICATION LOTTO

Objective

To match pictures

Materials

1. Colored bristol
2. Stickers of like subjects (fruits, pets, clothing, toys, tools, places, etc.)
3. Marking pens
4. Clear adhesive plastic

Making the Game

1. Rule the bristol board into squares.
2. Make small cards, the same size as the squares on the board.
3. Cover each square on the board with a different sticker.
4. Cover each small card with one identical sticker.
5. Cover all cards with clear plastic.

Playing the Game

1. Two or more players may play. Each player gets one card of a specific category.
2. The small cards are placed in a pile face down in the middle of the playing area.
3. Each player takes a turn picking a card from the pile.
4. If a player matches the card drawn, that player takes the card and covers the match. The player may then have a bonus turn.
5. The other players take their turns in order. The first to fill his/her card is the winner.

GO TOGETHER

Objective

To match pictures that share a relationship

Materials

1. Pictures of objects that share relationships: ball–bat, shoe–sock, hand–glove, garage–car, camera–film, hammer–nail, etc.

2. Bristol or tagboard

3. Clear plastic adhesive

Making the Game

1. Rule the board into 4" x 4" squares. Cut the squares.

2. Paste the pictures on the squares and cover with plastic.

Playing the Game

1. Spread all the cards out face up. Have the child choose any card. He/she then tries to find a card that could belong with the chosen card. When the child has chosen that particular card, he/she should have a reason why it was chosen rather than make a random guess.

2. After he/she has played the matching game, play "concentration" with the cards. Lay them all face down. The first player chooses a card and tries to guess where the match is. He/she turns a second card face up. If it matches, he/she may keep the pair, if not, he/she turns both cards over and the next player goes. The object is to remember where all the previous cards have been turned up in order to make matching easier. The one with the most pairs wins.

WHAT ANIMAL?

Objective

To categorize different types of animals

Materials

1. Stickers of various types of animals (farm, circus, and jungle); also pictures of pets and birds

2. Colored folding bristol or tagboard; cardboard is also needed

3. Waterbased felt markers

4. Clear plastic adhesive paper

Making the Game

1. Plan on having five or six rows of spaces on a gameboard, five spaces to a row. If you wish, you may also have left to right progression by having the player return to the left in order to begin each row. See diagram.

2. Alternate the three or four categories of stickers, making sure there is at least one bird in each row.

3. From the cardboard cut a 6" circle for a spinner. Divide the circle into eight sections. Alternate the three or four categories of animals and the birds so that two sections of each are represented.

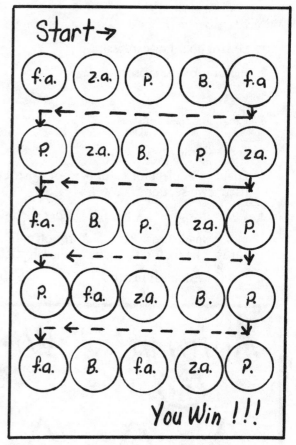

4. Cover the gameboard and spinner with the plastic. Use a paper fastener or a "buttoneer" plastic button fastener to attach the pointer.

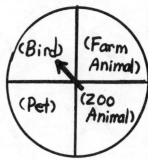

Playing the Game

1. Show the child the spinner and discuss the different categories on the spinner.

2. Each player takes a turn, spins the pointer and moves his/her marker along the board until the player reaches a space containing the type of animal the pointer stopped at. For example, if the pointer stopped at "farm animals," the player moves his/her marker until he/she comes to a space containing a farm animal.

3. If the pointer stops at "birds," however, the player must move his/her man backward until he/she comes to a space with a bird.

4. The player who lands on the last space first wins.

WHAT TIME OF YEAR IS IT?

Objective

To match holidays or activities that occur during the various seasons

Materials

1. Bristol board or cardboard
2. Pictures of the seasons
3. Paste
4. Clear plastic adhesive

Making the Game

1. Divide the piece of cardboard or bristol board into four sections or if only two sections are used, two sections.
2. Cut out four to six triangles under each season for holding small cards.
3. Make small cards. Paste pictures of holidays or activities familiar at individual seasons on the cards. The pictures may be found on stickers, in old workbooks, or in calendars.
4. Cover with clear plastic.

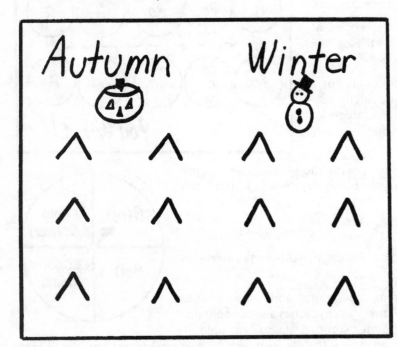

Playing the Game

1. Discuss the small cards with the child. (When does Halloween take place? When do leaves fall?) Also discuss the four seasons.

2. Have child place the small cards in the pocket under the correct season. Check the child's answer or the small cards may be color-coded on the back for self-checking (e.g., yellow for summer, etc.).

SHAPE MATRIX PUZZLE

Objective

To solve a problem by manipulating colored shapes to complete an arrangement

Materials

1. Bristol board
2. Marking pens
3. Shape stickers
4. Clear plastic adhesive
5. Small envelope

Making the Game

1. Use a 9" x 12" piece of bristol board. Divide this into sixteen squares.
2. Make a matrix puzzle with the shape stickers or by making colored shapes. Leave approximately nine squares blank.
3. Cut out small colored shapes that would complete the matrix puzzle.
4. Cover the card with plastic adhesive.

Playing the Game

1. Row by row, have the child discuss the shape and color he/she sees.
2. The child picks the small colored shapes to complete the puzzle, explaining why he/she is using that particular shape.
3. When completed, the first row should have a blue circle, a blue rectangle, a blue square, and a blue triangle. The other rows should follow the same colors and shapes.

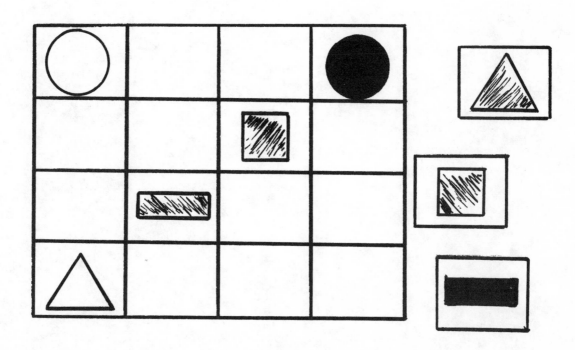

Seriation

BIG, BIGGER, BIGGEST

Objective

To be able to seriate according to size

Materials

1. Folding bristol
2. Marking pens
3. Scissors
4. Clear adhesive plastic
5. Ruler

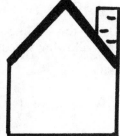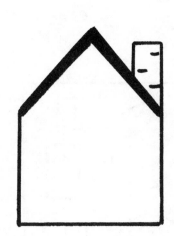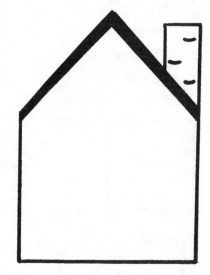

Making the Game

1. What you make depends on what you feel you can draw. Begin by making a graduated set of circles, triangles, squares, and rectangles, each set a different color, but all members of the set the same color (all circles blue, all squares red, etc.). The smallest would measure 2'', the largest 8'', making six graduated members of each set. Cover them with plastic before you cut them out.

2. For those who feel comfortable, make sets of houses, trees, Teddy bears, out of the bristol and decorate with the pens. Cover everything with plastic before you cut them out.

Playing the Game

1. Spread the circles out in random order. Always have the child work left to right. Have him place the circles in order, smallest to largest, largest to smallest.

2. Mix two different sets of shapes together and have the child sort them out, matching largest to largest; later have him match largest to smallest (large circle to smallest square).

BUILD THE TOWER

Objective

To introduce the concept of seriation

Materials

1. Bristol board 18" x 24"
2. Folding bristol
3. Ruler
4. Clear adhesive plastic
5. Marking pens
6. Drapery hooks
7. Hole punch

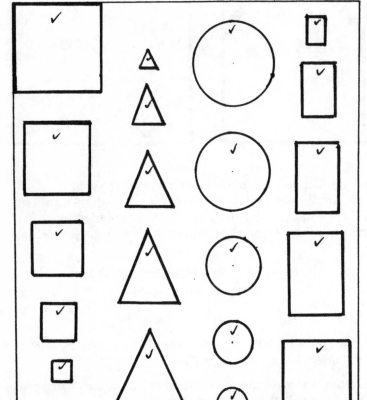

Making the Game

1. Using the folding bristol, make the following sets of shapes:

   Squares: 6", 5", 4", 3" and a 2" square

   Triangles: 6" h. with 6" base, 5" x 5", 4" x 4", 3" x 3", 2" x 2"

   Circles: 6", 5", 4", 3" and 2" diameter

   Rectangles: 6" x 5", 5" x 4", 4" x 3", 3" x 2", 2" x 1"

   Cover all the shapes with plastic before you cut them out.

2. Divide the bristol into four columns, 4½" x 24" each.

3. Trace each set of shapes onto the bristol following the illustration. Cover the bristol with plastic.

4. Place a drapery hook in each outlined shape. Punch a hole in each shape card.

Playing the Game

1. Stand the board up in the chalk tray.

2. Spread each set of shapes out on the playing area. Have the group find the first shape of the series and match it to the outline. If it fits, hang it on the hook. Match each set in order. Use the terms larger, smaller, largest, smallest.

CLOTHESLINE

Objective

To be able to seriate according to a specific characteristic

Materials

1. Length of rope, nails, hammer
2. Spring–type clothespins
3. Folding bristol
4. Sets of pictures for story sequencing, sets of letters for alphabet sequencing, sets of numbers, sets of objects
5. Clear adhesive plastic

Making the Game

1. Hang the clothesline in an area of the room where it can be left up for a few weeks.
2. Mount the pictures and sets of objects you will be using for seriating on the bristol and cover them with the plastic.

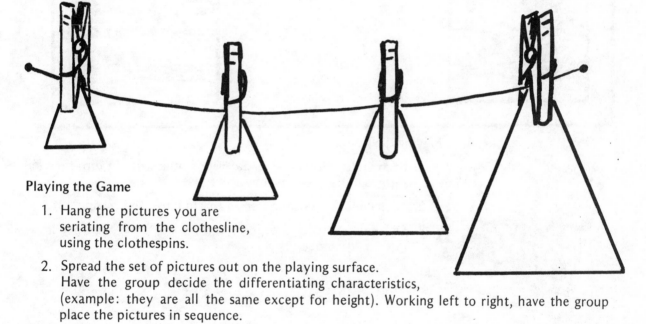

Playing the Game

1. Hang the pictures you are seriating from the clothesline, using the clothespins.
2. Spread the set of pictures out on the playing surface.
Have the group decide the differentiating characteristics,
(example: they are all the same except for height). Working left to right, have the group place the pictures in sequence.
3. A higher skill activity is to give the group ten letters of the alphabet from A to Z and have them place them in order.

THE FUNNIES

Objective

To develop the skill of sequencing

Materials

1. Comic strips

2. Scissors

3. Paste

4. Construction paper

Making the Game

1. This is an activity that is created by the children.

Playing the Game

1. Each child selects his/her favorite comic strip. In turn they tell the group the story as they see it.

2. Each child will cut the frames apart in his comic strip.

3. On the construction paper, the child will paste his story in sequence from memory.

THEN WHAT HAPPENED?

Objective

To develop the skill of sequencing, to seriate according to event

Materials

1. Manila envelope, 10" x 13"
2. Four-picture story (page from "readiness" workbook) — two identical pages
3. Folding bristol
4. Marking pen, scissors
5. Clear adhesive plastic

Making the Game

1. Cover the front of the envelope with colorful bristol. Divide the paper into four equal sections. In each section paste a picture of the story in sequence.
2. Cut a piece of bristol 4" x 18". Paste pictures from the duplicate page onto the bristol, 4" apart. Cover the pictures with plastic and cut them apart with curved lines to fit together later as a puzzle.
3. Cover the envelope with plastic and put the puzzle pieces inside.

Playing the Game

1. Look at the pictures on the envelope. Help the player make up a simple story. Go over the story a few times, discussing each picture.
2. Turn the envelope face down and take out the puzzle piece story. Spread out the four pictures and have the player select the picture in order of sequence. The puzzle pieces will fit if the pictures are chosen in sequence.

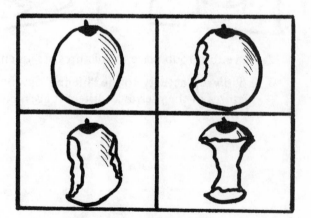

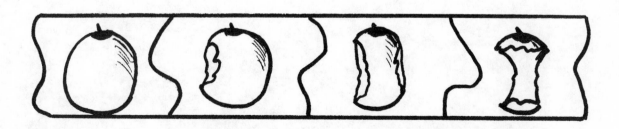

LIFELINE

Objective

To develop the skill of sequencing, to seriate according to time and age

Materials

1. Folding bristol, 18'' x 24'' long

2. Pictures of an infant, young child, teen-ager, young adult, middle-aged adult, elderly adult

3. Scissors

4. Clear adhesive plastic

Making the Game

1. Cut the paper 4'' wide by 18'' or 24'' long.

2. Paste the pictures on the paper in sequence, youngest to oldest, leaving a 4'' space between pictures.

3. Cover the pictures with plastic. Carefully cut the pictures apart using a curved line.

Playing the Game

1. Spread the pictures out randomly. Discuss each picture with the group. Relate the pictures to members of their families.

2. Have the group place the pictures in sequence, discussing the reasons for each of their choices.

3. Follow-up activity to the "lifeline" is a bulletin board display of the class's family pictures, pictures of themselves at different ages, pictures of the teacher at different ages.

FOLLOW THE PATTERN

Objective

To develop the skill of sequencing, to seriate according to a pattern

Materials

1. Folding bristol
2. Colorful sets of identical pictures of simple objects
3. Ruler
4. Clear adhesive plastic
5. Marking pens, pencil

Making the Game

1. The gameboard should be 6" x 12". 1" from the top of the board draw a row of three 1½" squares. 2" down from the top row, draw a row of eight 1½" squares (follow the illustration).

2. For the pattern cards, rule the paper into 1½" squares.

3. Place a different picture in each of the three top row squares. Use the same pictures to make eight pattern cards.

4. Outline the squares on the gameboard with a colorful pen.

5. Cover the gameboard and the cards with plastic, and cut the cards apart.

Playing the Game

1. Place the gameboard in the middle of the playing area. Have the player read the pattern in the top row out loud, left to right.

2. Spread out the eight pattern cards. Have the player duplicate the pattern row below on the empty spaces with the pattern cards.

3. For a higher level activity, cover the pattern row and have the player duplicate it from memory.

4. A lower skill game would be to have only two items in the pattern. Of course, you can make the gameboard larger, and have four items or more patterns, making the skill level higher.

Spatial

CHIPS ARE FUN

Objective

To be able to see spatial relationships

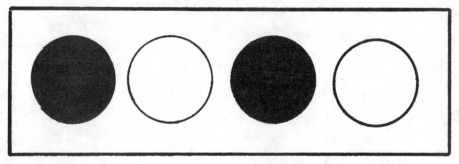

Materials

1. White folding bristol

2. Red, blue and black marking pens

3. Red, blue and white poker chips

4. Clear adhesive plastic

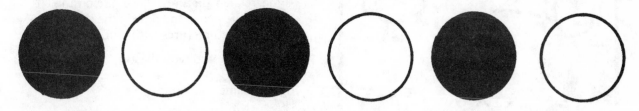

Making the Game

1. Rule the white bristol into 3" x 9" pattern cards.

2. Start with a simple two-color pattern (red, white, red, white). Trace around a poker chip to make the circle, and color in the circles. To indicate a white chip, trace with the black pen and do not color in the circle. Increase the difficulty of the patterns to fit your group.

3. Cover the cards with plastic and cut them apart.

Playing the Game

1. Choose a pattern card. Discuss it with the group, reading the pattern left to right.

2. Put out thirty chips, ten of each color.

3. Have the child place the chips directly on the card so that he/she may see how the chips correspond to the pattern circles.

4. Now, have the child remove the chips from the card and duplicate the pattern on the playing area below the card. Have him/her continue to repeat the pattern until all the chips are used.

5. A higher skill activity would be to have the player turn the pattern card face down and duplicate the pattern from memory.

TRACE AND FOLLOW

Objective

To develop left-to-right directional awareness

Materials

1. Folding bristol
2. Marking pens
3. Assortment of pictures
4. Clear adhesive plastic
5. Wax crayon

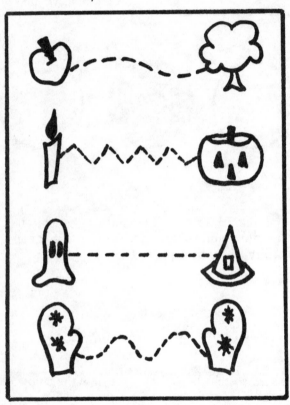

Making the Game

1. Find related pictures. Place one on the left side of the paper and one on the right. Connect the two pictures with a dotted line.

2. Cover the board with plastic.

Playing the Game

1. Have the child place the crayon on the picture on the left and trace the line to the object on the right.

2. Use a soft cloth to erase the crayon marks.

WHERE DO I PUT IT?

Objective

To develop specific spatial concepts

Materials

1. Bristol board, 24" x 18", folding bristol
2. Small drapery hooks
3. Marking pens
4. Assortment of pictures
5. Clear adhesive plastic
6. Hole punch

Making the Game

1. Draw the face of "bunny" in the center of the bristol. Color it with the marking pens. If you feel you absolutely cannot draw, use a simple, clear, colorful full page picture from a magazine. Cut it out and paste it in the middle of the bristol.

2. Cover the illustrated bristol with plastic.

3. Position the drapery hooks in the following places: directly above the picture, below the picture, two on the left side, and two on the right side (see illustration).

4. Rule the folding bristol into 3" x 3" cards. Place a picture on each card and cover with plastic. Make twelve cards. Punch a hole.

Playing the Game

1. Place the gameboard on the chalkboard so that it will stand upright.

2. Spread out the small cards. It is easier to introduce the position words in pairs and in different sessions. Some pairs you may choose to introduce are: over–under, above–below, beside–between, left–right, bottom–top.

3. Have each member of the group place a card according to your direction.

4. To introduce in front of–behind, make a second board with the picture in profile.

COPY MY COLOR

Objective

To develop directional awareness

Materials

1. White folding bristol
2. Marking pens
3. Ditto spirit masters
4. Clear adhesive plastic

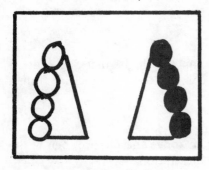

Making the Game

1. Decide on the concept you wish to teach — left-right, above-below, left diagonal-right diagonal.

2. Clue cards should be clear and simple. Let's start with left-right. Rule the bristol into 3'' x 4'' sections. Choose a simple design. Draw the design, one facing left and one facing right, on the card. Color them, using a different color for each design.

3. Cover the cards with plastic and cut them apart.

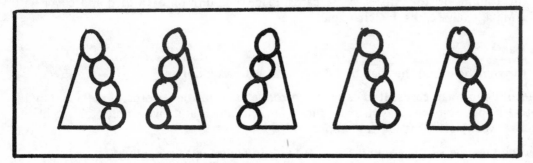

4. Make a corresponding ditto master for each design. Rule the master 4'' x 11''. Repeat the design, randomly changing from left to right.

Playing the Game

1. Have each member of the group choose a pattern card. Discuss it with the player. Talk about the colors. It will be your decision whether you will also introduce the vocabulary.

2. Give each child the corresponding ditto paper that matches his clue card and crayons. Starting on the left side, have him color the pictures according to their color on the clue card. (All the ones facing left will be blue, all the ones facing right will be red.)

Motor

SNIP, SNIP

Objective

To develop the fine motor skill of a one–cut scissor action

Materials

1. Ruler

2. Marking pen

3. Scissors

4. Colored construction paper

Making the Game

1. On the construction paper, rule 1" x 12" strips.

2. On each strip rule a line every inch.

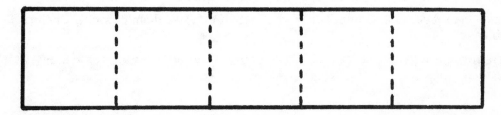

Playing the Game

1. Help the child to hold the scissors correctly, with his/her thumb on top.

2. Holding the strip of paper with one hand, have him/her cut the sections off with a one-cut snip of the scissors.

3. Save all the cut squares for an art project.

FRINGE IT

Objective

To develop the fine motor skill of cutting with scissors

Materials

1. Scissors
2. Construction paper

Making the Game

Cut the construction paper into shapes that correspond with your lessons, or with the season (example: pumpkins, trees, snowmen).

Playing the Game

1. To introduce the skill of fringing, give each child a pair of scissors and a 9" x 12" piece of construction paper. Demonstrate fringing by emphasizing that it is only a one–snip cut with the scissors. Encourage them to make the cuts close together.

2. Give each child the shape that corresponds to your activities. Have them decorate it before they begin to fringe.

3. Fringing is an ongoing activity that can be part of your art center. After they have drawn a picture, have them fringe it.

TRACING

Objective

To develop the fine motor skill needed to trace

Materials

1. Oaktag
2. Wide black marking pen
3. Clear adhesive plastic
4. Spring–type clothespins

Making the Game

1. Cut the oaktag to 8½" x 11". Draw a simple outline picture or shape with the black marker. Make sure the lines of your drawing are clear, simple, and few.

2. Cover the picture with plastic.

Playing the Game

1. We use mimeograph or ditto paper for the tracing paper. It is possible to see the picture through the paper, especially if you have used bold, dark lines in the drawing.

2. Demonstrate to the group how to attach the tracing paper to the tracing design. Use the clothespins to hold the paper firmly.

3. The child traces the design with a pencil or crayon.

LACING

Objective

To develop the fine motor skill needed to lace

Materials

1. Folding bristol
2. Child's coloring book with simple objects
3. Hole punch
4. Marking pens
5. Long colored shoelace or skatelace
6. Clear adhesive plastic

Making the Game

1. Each lacing card will measure approximately 9" x 12". You may draw a simple picture (apple, jack-o-lantern, fish, house, teddy bear, ball, etc.) on the bristol and cut out the shape. If you do not wish to draw, cut out a large simple picture from the coloring book, paste it to the bristol and cut around the picture again. Color the picture before you cover it with the plastic. Cover both sides with plastic.
2. Punch holes all around the edge of the card.

Playing the Game

1. Knot the lace for each card. Demonstrate to the group how to lace.

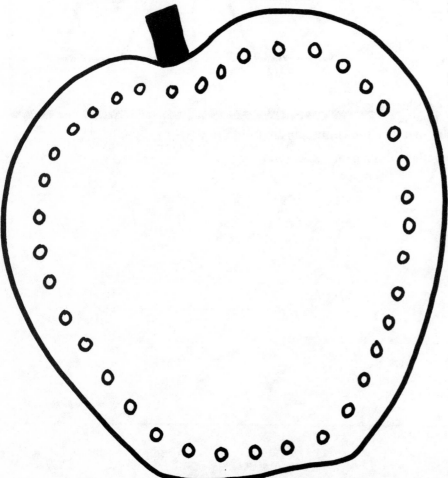

2. Have each child choose a lacing card. Sit with the group to assist to limit frustration.
3. Cut lacing cards from construction paper.

   Knot sturdy yarn and wrap tape around the end of the yarn. Use pictures to illustrate your lessons (example: children lace "egg" shape to relate to "Humpty Dumpty," "stop signs for your safety lesson).

TWIST IT

Objective

To develop small muscles needed for fine motor activities

Materials

1. Assorted sizes of screws and nuts
2. Plastic bag

Making the Game

None

Playing the Game

1. Spread the screws and nuts out on the playing area.
2. The player will fit the screws and nuts together by trial and error.
3. When he/she has fitted all the screws to the nuts, the player will unscrew each pair. Make sure the player is using his thumb and forefinger.

WALNUT GAME

Objective

To develop small muscle control

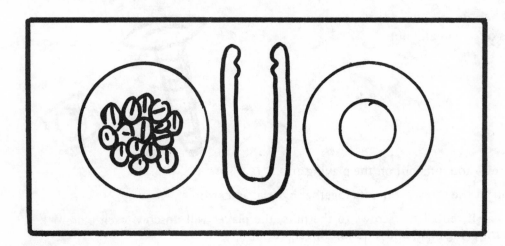

Materials

1. Two plastic bowls, different colors
2. Tongs
3. Walnuts
4. Tray

Making the Game

1. Place bowls on the tray with tongs.

2. Put eight walnuts in one bowl.

Playing the Game

1. Demonstrate to the group how to transfer the nuts, one at a time, from one bowl to the other.

2. Have the children work from left to right and then right to left.

MAGIC SHOE

Objective

To develop the fine motor skill of shoe tying

Materials

1. Heavy bristol board
2. Marking pens
3. Scissors
4. Shoelace
5. Piece of felt
6. Metal eyelets, eyelet punch
7. Clear adhesive plastic
8. Stapler

Making the Game

1. Outline the shoe on the bristol. It should measure approximately 9" x 4". Cut out the shoe. Color the shoe with the pens. Cover it with the plastic.

2. Cut two pieces of felt to fit the indicated spaces. Staple to the shoe. Punch holes and attach the metal eyelets to the pieces of felt.

3. Color-code each end of the shoelace with red and blue.

Playing the Game

1. Give each player in the group his/her own shoe and shoelace. Demonstrate each step to the group and have the group imitate.

2. The color-coded laces will enable the group to follow it better.

3. To limit frustration, being able to lace a lacing card easily is a good entry behavior for this skill.

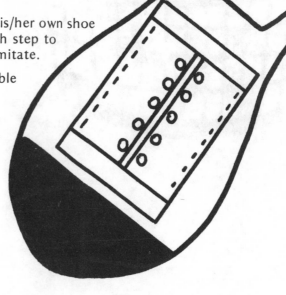

CLOTHESPIN DROP

Objective

To develop eye–hand coordination for fine motor activities

Materials

1. Large mouth plastic bottle
2. "Old-fashioned" clothespins (no spring)
3. Small laundry basket

Making the Game

Place the bottle in the center of the basket.

Playing the Game

1. Demonstrate to the group how to drop the clothespins into the bottle. Have the children stand up while dropping the pins.

2. Make two sets of clothespins by coloring them with a pen. The team that has the most pins in the bottle at the end is the winner.